Nobody Knows Tomorrow

About the Author

Joseph Egwurube is a Nigerian who resides in France. He was born in 1957. He currently teaches at the Faculty of Law, Political Science and Management at La Rochelle University but enjoys creative writing, especially poems, which he shares with his university colleagues. Educated in Zaria in Nigeria and Bordeaux in France, where he obtained a Doctorate degree in Political Science, he spent several years teaching as a Senior Lecturer at Ahmadu Bello University, Zaria, in Nigeria before moving to settle in France. A few of his poems have been published in Teaching Times, the France TESOL Magazine.

Joseph Egwurube

Nobody Knows Tomorrow

Olympia Publishers
London

www.olympiapublishers.com
OLYMPIA PAPERBACK EDITION

A CIP catalogue record for this title is
available from the British Library.

ISBN: 978-1-80074-320-5

First Published in 2022

Olympia Publishers
Tallis House
2 Tallis Street
London
EC4Y 0AB
Printed in Great Britain

Dedication

For my dear mother, Ogaba Anya Christiana Enatta
Egwurube, for showing us, her children, the example and the
way forward, and for my two sons, Mimi and Jojo,
for their patience and understanding.

Acknowledgements

This work has come through thanks to the support of two women. First, Joëlle "Miss Goodwine" Bonnevin, a rare gem, a very reliable life companion and friend, who believed in my writing project and encouraged me to go the whole hog. Secondly, Catherine Walter, a very dependable friend indeed, who painstakingly proof-read the initial draft and made many useful comments and corrections.

1

"The mistress of my house," beckoned a quiet voice, full of authority. The voice belonged to someone who was visibly used to people doing his bidding. It rose from a large wooden bed in the private NAKOWA clinic in Funtua, a medium-sized city in the north of Nigeria, where a frail unshaved old man, wearing a multi-coloured wrapper around his waist lay, panting slowly for breath. He had no shirt on, and his chest, moist and studded with a light crop of grey hair, was heaving silently up and down. The man's face was slightly emaciated, his cheeks slightly sunken, bones sticking out, but his eyes were fiery and alive and had a questioning look. "Can you hear me or do I have to shout for you to answer?"

An elderly woman was sitting on a chair close to the bed. She was in deep thoughts. The man and the woman were both in one of the three suites, on the top floor of the private clinic. These wards were presented as suites because each of them was occupied by only one patient at a time, much unlike the others which had several beds lined against the walls. Each suite had a flush toilet and a sink with tap water in a separate room attached to it. Their occupants were therefore privileged because they could go to ease themselves whenever they felt the need, without the anxiety of waiting uncomfortably for long minutes in the queue that regularly formed before the single toilet located at the extremity of the floor. This particular suite was sparsely furnished. Apart from the double wooden bed with a Dunlopillo mattress on which the man lay, there was also a closed wooden cupboard, a medium-sized square plastic table on which there was a worn Bible with many torn pages placed under a white unlit table lamp, two white plastic chairs, including the one on which the woman silently sat, and a small wooden stool. It was getting close to six in the evening, the room was hot and a white wobbling ceiling fan had been turned on. The fan was not rotating rapidly and it seemed to squeak now and then. There was a light fresh odour of antiseptic in the air because the corridor on the floor had been cleaned a while ago with a bucket of water mixed with Dettol. The woman, dressed in worn and stained Ankara clothes, had been sitting close to the bed for over five hours, in very deep thoughts, and quite unaware of what was happening elsewhere in the clinic. She was waiting for her husband to wake up after having been sedated to sleep at noon. She had tried then unsuccessfully to feed him but he had refused to eat because he said he had other things on his mind than eating. He seemed to have lost appetite. She sat there silently, patiently waiting, and praying. Outside, one could hear the noise of the electric generator that had been switched on earlier on in the morning when NEPA, the National Electric Power Authority, had cut power, as it usually did every day. The clinic was a two-storey building with a total of seven wards on the upper floor and several offices on the ground floor. It was on the ground floor that most of its activities were organised. There was an Emergency/Registration Room with a large ageing computer and a filing cabinet, a Maternity/Paediatrics Room where a group of nurses were always prompt to answer the questions of worried mothers and try to calm down crying babies, an

Operating Room with a stretcher, a Pharmacy that always smelt of iodine and the Medical Doctor's Office where all consultations took place. The clinic belonged to the third son of the man and the elderly woman. After obtaining his medical degree at the University of Nsukka in Eastern Nigeria, Dr Clement Ubah had decided that private medical practice was a quick way to make money while being independent. Northern Nigeria was where the need for medical attention would grow dramatically, he had thought. The choice of Funtua had been well calculated: there was not a single clinic there, so Doctor Ubah knew he'd have the whole city to himself. What is more, Funtua was only an hour's drive from Zaria, where there was a university teaching hospital to which he could eventually send cases he'd find difficult to resolve.

The sound of a child crying in one of the wards came to the attention of the woman, who could now hear the doctor responding to the thanks being expressed profusely by another woman. He was in a ward where three patients were lodged. Two had been admitted for more than a week but the doctor was speaking to the mother of a four-year old girl who had been rushed in the night before with headache, nausea and sweating. The doctor had prescribed some quinine tablets and he was now reassuring the anxious mother that the malaria fever that had attacked her daughter was by God's grace almost vanquished.

"How is your body, Ogaba Idu," the woman answered in a subdued voice.

Her thoughts flew back quickly to what her life had been three days earlier. She had woken up as usual in the village, more than five hundred kilometres away from Funtua, to do her daily chore, ensure that the compound was swept, that the big green jerrycans had water in them and that all would be ready for the important events that would happen during the day. A few women had woken up almost at the same time as she had, and had come to greet her with due respect. She was referred to mostly as "Ogaba Anya" in her capacity as the wife of the village head, but sometimes people called her "Ene Ole" (the house mistress) or a more generic "Mama." Her husband, who had been made District Head by the State government, had called for an important meeting of the Council of Chiefs in his parlour that afternoon, and she needed to make sure those invited would be received with due regard. It was unthinkable for members of the council, especially the "Ada Agila" (Prime Minister) or the "Otse Arekwu" (the Religious Guide), to come to the village head's home and not leave with their stomachs full and their thirsts quenched. It was a question of not losing face and this she accepted as a duty never to fail, as her role to ensure. She had gone into one of the rooms where the boys slept, to wake Otsege, the houseboy, up. Some chickens had to be slaughtered and the fire in the open yard, that served as kitchen, lit to prepare the jollof rice that would be served during the meeting which had been convened to discuss how to resolve the looming crisis between the Ezas, of Ibo extraction, and the inhabitants of the village over land rights. An Eza man had been caught by a villager, whose brother had been killed a week earlier by others in an Eza market, and the bereaved villager had wanted to behead him in retaliation. The Eza had been arrested and it was decided that only the village head could determine the man's fate as was the custom. It was not the first time such a crisis situation had cropped up. This time however, her husband, who had complained a day earlier of incessant pains in the chest and of how he was finding it difficult to find his words, wondered if he would be able to remain calm over the vociferous debate he knew would greet his decision to let the Eza man go unharmed, as he had decided in all previous occasions. He had always warned his councillors of the dire consequences that would follow a hard-line an-eye-for-an-eye approach in solving such inter-communal antagonisms. As a pot with holes full of water would sink if left to flow on a stream, so would Eza villagers come to avenge their sons and daughters killed by us, he would say calmly before the elders. It seemed that a few members of the Council of Chiefs expected him to be more offensive, more threatening and less accommodating.

"This cannot go on forever," one of the councillors had said. "We cannot continue to allow them to trample on us, behead our brothers, occupy our land, and destroy our farms when they so decide without letting them know that we own the land. The stranger who touches your body and afterwards licks his fingers while looking directly into your eyes will wait for your death before he comes to eat you up."

"What you say sits very well in my mind," another had insisted. "The other day, I was in the market and was discussing with one of the Eza yam sellers. Can you imagine my total surprise when another Eza man interrupted our discussion and started speaking with the yam seller in their language without a simple 'Good morning' or 'Good afternoon' in my direction! Wonders will never end, I tell you. A man needs to sweep his house himself if he wants to kill the scorpion that is hiding in one corner of the house."

"Maybe in their place, they don't say 'Good morning' or 'Good afternoon' to people they don't know."

"May I however remind you that it is not only the Ezas

that refuse to say, 'Good morning' or 'Good afternoon' to people," another councillor had interjected. "I know of many Agila men who think they have made it, or that they are very well-educated and who always pretend not to recognise you when they cross you on the road."

"That is quite true," added a fourth councillor. "Wonders will never end. Some children have grown small beards and believe it is the elders that have to greet them first."

"What do you expect when all they do is smoke and listen to music on the radio all day, rather than go to the farm with their parents? What kind of education are we giving them, I ask?"

"I agree with you. My neighbour and relative was telling me the other day that the nephew he had accepted to bring up in his home not only refuses to wake up early in the morning to help clean the compound but always drags his feet when told to go and fetch water from the Igbilede stream. When he finishes eating, he doesn't say 'thank you' to us like our proper children do, or offer to help wash the cooking pot or plates."

"What is happening to our descendants? Where have all their manners gone?"

"Well, you cannot expect a chick to know how to pick worms without learning one or two lessons from the cock. We cannot continue to complain as if the fault is not ours in the first place," someone ventured to add. "It is not in my house that a child will not know he or she is a child."

"Why should we always blame ourselves? Did our fathers and mothers not bring us up the way we are trying to bring up those who are following us? Did we not learn that one of the basic things in life is to greet people, even if they have wronged us? Wonders will never end, I tell you once more," someone else had continued.

"Well, it is not only children who have forgotten their manners. There are some who have become very rich and who think that good manners can either be bought or else be forgotten altogether. When they decide to speak to you, they give you the impression that they are doing you a great favour. They speak but never listen to what you say or answer the questions you ask them. All they tell you is where and how they lived in Lagos or Ibadan or Kano or Enugu, or what schools their children are attending in the North, in the West or in the East," another councillor added.

"Speaking of those who have wronged us and who will continue to wrong us until we tell them 'Stop!', what do we do?" interjected the councillor who had spoken first. "Do we meekly give them the other cheek for them to slap us until they are tired, or do we tell them 'Stop' in the only language they know? A dead elephant cannot ward off flies that hover over it."

Despite the usual debate concerning the most appropriate choice to make, and the strong disagreement expressed by a few hardliners on the non-violent response the District Head had decided, the meeting had fortunately gone well, the Eza man had been left to go unharmed and to be a messenger of goodwill from Agila to his community and the councillors were being served their jollof rice, fried chicken and drinks and were chatting boisterously, arguing about who was the best dancer when they were all younger and comparing the number of yam tubers each had harvested from their farms recently. The village drummer was beating his goat-skinned drum excitedly to a larger number of people because a few non-royal elders had come to partake of the meal that Ogaba Anya was offering to the village notables. There was laughter and loud talk in the parlour. It was unexpected of the District Head to eat in the presence of the others, so his meal had been served in his bedroom. She had gone in to give him some drinking water when she saw how still he was sitting on his armchair, having difficulty breathing. She had immediately spoken quietly to the Ada Agila, phoned Funtua, and had the driver of the Land Rover called from his home and asked to make arrangements to quickly and discreetly leave the village later in the day.

"Can you hear the noise that is about to happen," the voice continued in a low, almost inaudible, whisper.

"There is no noise that I hear, Ogaba Idu, father and master of the house," the woman continued.

"Oh, I keep on forgetting that you are a woman. Of course, a very loud noise is about to be made. At the moment, there are three men in the room who are preventing me from eating. Can't you see them?"

"There is no one in this room apart from you and me."

"Unbelievable! Okay. I won't stop you from being a woman. Of course, there are three men here now. They were sent by my enemies in the village to prevent me from eating. Peace be to the village. I don't know if I will be able to go back to the village soon. This illness I have, I don't know where it comes from. Last night, I was invited to a very large white room with lots of adjacent offices. The room looked very familiar, as if I had been there before. There were many people who looked very familiar, all of them dressed in white agbadas. The headman, who was very thin but tall, with white beards and very white teeth came to me, offered me some kola nuts and showed me my office. He said the office would be there waiting for me."

"You must be very tired to be speaking like this. You know you are not going anywhere for the meantime. Do you want me to stay in the room and keep you company until you are hungry enough to eat what has been prepared for you? There is very warm akamu and hot akara. And there is Bournvita too if you are thirsty. You need to eat to remain strong. Do not forget that the cassava bread is never too hot for a hungry and empty stomach. You will sleep better when you eat because we all know that the eyes cannot close and sleep when the stomach is not asleep too," the woman replied. "If you want me to remain in the room with you tonight, this I will do willingly, Oga," she continued.

"Ehe, so now you want to sleep on the king's bed, abi? Do you think your presence will stop what has been ordained from happening?"

"It is normal for a wife to wish her husband well and to stand by him always," she said.

"You are a woman, but you are intelligent. Or maybe you are trying to draw my attention to the fact that she is not here at the clinic with me. When I go, will you forgive her?" he continued.

"When you go where, and me to forgive who?"

"Forgive Mama Baby, Sonny's mother."

"Forgive her for what?"

He avoided the woman's eyes and kept quiet for what seemed an eternity. Sonny's mother was his second wife. She was aware of her husband's illness but had seemed totally unaffected by what was happening to him. She had decided long ago not to live under the same roof with him anymore and no one knew why she had made such a choice. There was talk around the village that she was a witch, but she was unaffected by such talk. That her husband had been transported urgently to a clinic far away in the North and was being treated for an illness no one could name did not seem to bother her at all. What would her presence around him add or subtract from his wellbeing or the rapidity with which he would get better, she was reported to have said when a group of elders had told her to follow her husband rather than stay behind doing iyanga like tolotolo? The man would ask everyday if any call had been made by her to the clinic and if so why no one had bothered to wake him up to take the calls. He had been told the truth each time, but he would always try to justify Sonny's mother's absence and attitude by saying she was, without any doubt, busy with one thing or the other where she was. He would remind those around him to transfer the call he knew would soon come to him immediately it was made.

"I do not want to quarrel with you. What I'm asking is if you will make sure there is peace in the house. Each time my children meet under my name, make sure they do not remain divided."

"Well, it is not me who divided them, and you know it."

"Like I said, I do not want to quarrel with you. What I'm doing is that I'm begging you and asking you for forgiveness. You have always been the Ene Ole, the mistress of the house. I'm entrusting the entire family to your care and hands. Let peace be the guiding principle. Please."

2

The elderly woman's name is Comfort Enotse. Like many of the inhabitants in her village, Agila, she has two first names, one native and traditional, the other Christian and western. Most villagers know and understand where their native first names come from and what they mean but few are able to explain, even when they have advanced education, the origins and meanings of their Christian names.

Her traditional name, used only by her age mates and people older than her when addressing her, comes from her paternal grandmother whom she unfortunately never knew. She had had a total of twelve children, before passing way to the land of Arekwus, the community of departed elders. She had been a very vocal woman, never shy and never hesitating to speak during public gatherings or community meetings. She would always say what was on her mind although this was frowned upon by the elders in the village, most of whom thought a woman should normally dance rather than jump, meaning she should not attract undue attention to herself. Such common thoughts hardly impressed the grandmother who would sometimes be the first to give her opinion when the floor was open during communal gatherings. The elders could do nothing to stifle her because her voice was gold. She was the village singer and could produce the lyrics of different songs to fit different circumstances of life at very short notice. She was extremely creative. It was to her that people went when they had marriages to celebrate, when the birth of a first son had to be 'washed' as the saying went, or when the community gathered at the end of a very bountiful harvest to thank the ancestors for bringing the rain and keeping off the locusts. She was therefore depended on. It was reported that she was so independent in thoughts, spirit and actions that she did not hesitate to question decisions taken by the council of elders once or twice when the village was bent on going to war with another village.

Her fame had been increased by the life of her second child, Agbo Ochoga, father to Enotse. Agbo Ochoga, had been a strong powerfully built man. He never smiled, never had time to play with his children, never wasted time on what he considered unimportant things like telling stories, always seemed to be in a hurry to finish one thing or the other. When he woke up very early in the morning, he would first eat what had been left over from the supper of the preceding day, usually fufu or pounded yam with dried okra soup. Only the soup was warmed. He would then silently spend long minutes sharpening his cutlass and hoe before leaving for the farm. He would take along with him a piece of yam, one or two cassavas, some salt and some palm oil all of which he would use for lunch in his farm. Agbo Ochoga's nightmare was to be unable to provide enough for his family to eat. When sometimes people told him he worked too much, he would respond that it was not the neighbour's hoe that would finish tilling his land and provide for his family. Agbo Ochoga had been an accomplished hunter and farmer and had succeeded in obtaining the chieftaincy title, Agama Agila. The Agama Agila was thus an "otse" or chief, which is why his mother was referred to afterwards as "Ene Otse" or the mother of the chief, a name that stuck.

Agbo Ochoga had risen to become one of the most influential members of the Council of Chiefs, the Agila Traditional Council, since he was empowered as the foreign relations chief to determine and manage the relations between Agila and its neighbours. Most of these were Ibo communities established close to Agila village which belonged to the Idoma tribe. The Agama Agila usually had his hands full because the relationship between Agila and the neighbouring Ibo communities, which were short of arable land and so were always expanding their farmlands into territories that had belonged for a long time to Agila farmers, were quite antagonistic. Clashes between Agila and Eza Ibo communities were therefore very frequent.

Enotse was her father's first child and daughter. She was told that her birth had been well received by her father, the Agama, because he knew he would be given a heavy dowry when her time to depart his home would come. Some stories had it that in reality, the Agama had wanted his first child to be a son but Enotse's birth was without doubt a moment of joy for her mother, Ochiba Ogezi. One of the many songs the mother used to sing when she asked her daughter to follow her to the stream to fetch water was:

The gods of Agila be thanked
For giving me my husband's mother
I can now patiently wait for my old age to come
Because I know my mother will be there to feed me
To hold my hands
To wash my face and body
And lighten the burden of living

She will give me several grandchildren
For the Ochoga household to show to the world
The wealth in numbers
And the pride in being a big and united family
A single wall does not constitute a house
The jaws do not eat if the legs do not move and advance
A single piece of wood generates smoke but does not give fire
As one hand is needed to wash the other
So will the Ochoga family be ever together
Full of joy, health and wealth

Enotse showed much promise as a young girl. She would wake up earlier than others in the compound to sweep it and would then wait for her mates to wake up before they trekked to the stream with large clay pots and calabashes to fetch water for their respective families. She played mother with her brothers, sisters, cousins and relatives. She helped her mother do the cooking, always volunteered to go to the market to buy what was needed, never refused when she was sent on one errand or the other and was never seen playing with her age mates. Enotse's mother was very proud of her but never told her this.

Agila is a village in Nigeria. It is sandwiched between Ebonyi State, Enugu State and Igumale, which is the headquarters of Ado Local government to which it belongs. It was one of the first Idoma villages to come into contact with European missionaries. One Sunday morning, the town crier visited all the compounds asking all the villagers to assemble in the market square. The news was that a white father, called Father Patrick, had come to the village to bring it very good tidings and sow the seeds of community growth and general wellbeing. This was years before Nigeria obtained independence in 1960. Young Enotse, who was then about twelve years old, was like all her age mates curious to see a white man for the first time in the village. When she got to the market square, a very large crowd had already gathered. There was excited talk as the crowd's attention was focused not only on the reverend Father but also on a white Volkswagen Beetle car that was parked under the enormous locust bean tree at the centre of the square. The locust bean tree was where most village meetings were held, elders using the now polished big roots of the tree that protruded above the soil as seats. The villagers who were gathered around the tree were amazed at the sight before them, at the whiteness of the man and the whiteness and spotlessness of his car. Father Patrick, who was quite plumb, was dressed in a very white neat soutane that fell to his feet. He was wearing a pair of brown Bata sandals and white socks on his feet. He had a small white beret on his head, but some of his whitish hair could be seen bristling under the hot village sun, moving slightly back and forth with the light wind that was blowing. His face was impassive, and it was impossible from afar to see his eyes. He was sweating and was using a small white towel to regularly dab his face. He said nothing, waiting for those gathered around him to become quiet and attentive before he began his speech.

"Wonderful! So Oyibo man no get legs? How many feet and fingers he get?"

"Amazing! See as he get very pointed nose. How can he be able to breathe with such small nostrils?"

"If he no get legs, how he go drive his moto?"

"I hear say his car na automatic. He dey change gear himself and he go break when Oyibo man tell am to stop."

"How can somebody be white like this? He resemble

anjenu, those wey dey come from burial ground to deal with people who don do many bad things."

"Na true you dey talk. Maybe we must leave now now before he begin his long grammar."

"Wetin you dey yab, my sister? Make we no leave yet. I hear say he want build primary school here for us and to make connection between us and the district govment. Make we stay, hear his grammar, I beg."

There was a frenzy as well as apprehension everywhere as people were wondering what the father was going to say, in what language he was going to do this, and how all those gathered around him were going to understand him. It was then that a very handsome young man, the son of the Otse Arekwu, the religious guide and member of the Council of Chiefs in charge of masquerades, as well as being the messenger of spirits and departed ancestors, stood up at the centre of the market square and told everyone to quieten down. He was dressed not in wrappers as most of his age mates were, but in brown shorts and a white singlet. He went on to say that Agila village was lagging behind many neighbouring Ibo villages because it had not a single primary school or a Roman Catholic church. For him, this was the main reason why most of the stores in the village were owned by Ibos, and why it was to the Ibos that villagers turned when they wanted to write letters to members of their families living in Otukpo, the district headquarters. Father Patrick, who had left his country to help others, was kind enough to come to the aid of the village, to give the village the light, and to help it catch up with its more developed and civilised Ibo speaking neighbours, he went on to say. He was prepared to translate Father Patrick's message to the villagers, the new flock. He reminded the crowd that the white man's voice did not have any more secrets for him since he was studying in the Secondary School in nearby Utonkon city. There, not only were all the courses taught in English, the language that would be used by the father, but in addition he was proud to announce that one of the courses he took in Utonkon, for which he was always the best student with the highest mark, was Bible Knowledge.

"May peace and heavenly light fall here and now on this village in the name of the Father, the Son and the Holy Spirit, Amen," the Father began. "I can see the work of the Devil left, right and centre here in this village. I can smell lots of evil in this village. I can hear evil spirits planning on what to do so that the darkness that has engulfed you will never disappear. I am told that many of you engage in sacrificing animals and using many other ungodly means when you face temporary difficulties rather than believing in the power of the Almighty. I am aware that many of you do not understand such simple laws like 'You shall not steal' or 'You shall not have idols' or 'You shall not work on Sundays' or 'You shall not commit adultery'. You do all these things because you do not know, so of course the Lord Almighty, given his mercy, will willingly forgive your trespasses if you stop doing them immediately and if you accept henceforth to devote your life to his glory and ministry. The first and foremost thing that you should all do is to be baptised. You will then have a name that will give you solace and bring you closer to eternal light and life. There is no time to waste because the more you wait, the more power to the Devil and his advocates you will give. When you are baptised, I will give you the blessing that will permit you to have access to unlimited spiritual wealth and health and the strength that will enable you to make all the necessary effort to bring you closer to God the Father, the Son and the Holy Spirit, Amen. There is no time to waste."

Many of the villagers wanted wealth and health and so they joined a queue that was formed in less than ten minutes for the reverend Father to do a mass baptism ceremony. A list of possible names was given by the priest. Boys or men could choose one of twelve names: David, John, James, Joseph, Mathew, Michael, Christopher, Patrick, Pius, Paul, Peter and Gabriel. Girls or women could equally choose one of twelve names: Mary, Comfort, Josephine, Christiana, Catherine, Bridget, Patricia, Elizabeth, Helen, Abigail, Mercy and Victoria. Those willing to be baptised were informed that they could add other Christian names when they would be confirmed Christians. Most of these thus believed that their baptism meant they were going to undergo a trial period to see if they were worthy of joining the new community of God's chosen people. Father Patrick needed to be obeyed if the wealth and health that were promised were to be obtained.

Enotse was impressed by everything that happened that day. She was impressed by the presence of the white man and how he seemed to speak in a tongue that sounded strange but captivating. She was impressed by the young man who was capable of understanding such a strange language and of being able to say what the white man thought and expressed, without hesitating a single minute. How come he is able to anticipate what the white man is thinking, to be able to say the same thing like him, she wondered? How does it feel to have the right to transmit and translate the words of the white man's god? Was this the language taught at the secondary school in Utonkon? Did the teachers there teach people how to speak without breathing, as it appeared the white Father and the Agila boy were doing with ease? She was impressed by everything that happened that day and especially by the prospect of what was clearly written on the wall as her future, full of wealth and health, if she became baptised and if after passing the test, became later confirmed as a Christian. She therefore chose to be baptised Comfort, though she never enquired what the name meant.

Comfort Enotse had never been to any formal school. Her parents, like the parents of most of the girls in the village, did not think it necessary to send her to school because they did not feel it was important for girls to have formal Western education. It was common knowledge that girls would first become women, then later married women who would follow their husbands. Was it not said that when the water level decreases in the river, the fish chooses to remain inside rather than outside the water? In addition, the girls would have to walk many miles to attend school in a neighbouring Ibo village. This would take them long hours of walking, doing nothing, while important chores in their respective compounds were left unattended to. Similarly, it was believed that going to school meant reading and understanding the Bible and people did not know how such an education could be useful to a woman, to her family, to her compound and to the village in general. Would knowledge of the Bible teach the woman when to stop talking and listen to her parents or to her husband? Was it really necessary to try to allow the woman to learn the secrets of the white man's god when those of the gods of the village were forbidden to the same women because of their acknowledged status as being, unlike men, unable to differentiate between form and substance, between today and tomorrow, between dream and reality? Finally, and this was perhaps the overriding reason, no man in his right senses stomached the idea of having a wife who could read the Bible, speak like the white man and maybe know things that were unknown by her husband. Was it not the good husband that made it possible for the wife to be good? Could the woman have independence of thought without the guidance of the man, the father or the husband? Would a woman able to speak long grammar like the men who had gone to school not start to think she was the owner of the house? Did the elders not say that the small bed can never receive two people at the same time, meaning the woman had to wait to be invited rather than think she shared ownership with the man? Did the very intelligent elders, who had lots of experience, not say that the man is the root of prosperity in the house while the woman is only the mistress? Enotse's parents, and especially her father, the Agama Agila, an influential local notable, tried to bring up their female children governed by these beliefs.

Rather than go to school, she therefore stayed in the village and followed the path taken by all her age mates. Girls were organised in age grades and she was a member of the Ayi Ochiba age grade. The Ayi Ochiba age grade consisted of twelve teenage girls. They considered themselves as sisters and always cooperated in doing such chores as going to the river to fetch water or wash clothes. During the Ujo or new yam festival, they dressed in the same colourful Akwete clothes and sang during the wrestling matches that always concluded it. The Ayi Ochiba was a sort of school where Enotse learnt how to communicate with others, where she learnt patience, where she learnt that there was force in being with others always. Her mates considered her the most reasonable of them all because she never quarrelled with anyone. She never complained about anything. She never insulted anybody. She never got angry with any soul. She became the spokesperson of the group and it was her responsibility to get into contact with the equivalent age grade of the men, the Ayi Ebakwu, when there was a collective community work to be done. Members of the Ayi Ebakwu were very famous as hunters. Each time they went on a hunting expedition, they never came back empty handed. They would come back to the village to the tune of the following song:

Whose eyes are as sharp as those of the Ayi Ebakwu I ask
Nobody I must answer
Who walks as still as the Ayi Ebakwu I ask
No one I must answer
The antelope trembles
Each time the Ayi Ebakwu set foot in the bush
And the mouth of the village waters
In anticipation of the feast that is announced
The soup will become delicious
With the big piece of meat
That each Agila child can chew
And chop and chew and chop
Until the Ayi Ebakwu to the savanna return
For another round of unlimited eating to begin

A few people therefore saw Enotse as an illiterate woman because she had not been to school. She had not had the experience of carrying a slate with her always, on which she wrote the tables of multiplication one after the other with a piece of chalk, reciting each multiplication table automatically without even thinking. "Two times one is two, two times two

31

is four, two times three is six, two times four is eight…" In reality, she did not need formal multiplication tables to know how to count, how to add, how to subtract and how to multiply. Her main worry was not how to count or multiply. Her main worry was her fear not to be able to bear children. Such a prospect haunted her and so she felt that if she was kind to everyone, and especially to children, she would never become barren. It was believed in the village that barren women were ordained to be harlots or ashawos. These were very easy women with no morals and no respect for themselves and their families. When they went to the market with their flat bellies, young men around them would exchange knowing glances and happy mothers would greet them with hostility. The ashawos were considered as shameless women who brought shame to their parents and compounds. It was the last thing Enotse wanted to bring to her parents and compound: shame, losing face and a bad reputation.

In addition, Enotse believed that life could not always be a story of ups only. She was thus prepared to face a few downs, since she felt these would provide her with the opportunity to learn more about herself and about others. What was the use in complaining when things went wrong, since it was inevitable that such wrong moments would not last and would be followed by better ones? Anyhow, wrong moments were moments you could not control. What was the use of complaining about something you could not control? Rather than complain and wait for others to solve your problems for you, she would think, why not see problems and wrong moments as a way to test your resolve, as a gift to better yourself, as an avenue to change some things you do or how you do them, she would conclude. Enotse therefore felt that life needed to be lived now, today, and here. Focusing on problems rather than on non-problems was not a very viable and comfortable manner of living, especially if one had the gift of being able to have children, to found a family and to patiently wait for old age, since one would never be alone ever. Life seeps slowly away when you are busy being unhappy rather than acknowledging the joy of family life, of raising children, of having a husband, of having in-laws that drop by daily to ask about how you are doing, she would add to her reflections. A small voice in her mind would occasionally interrupt her thinking and question the wisdom in focusing always on living now and not planning for the future. How can you have a good husband and lots of children if you do not search for them, and if you do not diligently work to have a happy life, the voice would say. If you are the only girl not to work actively to be recognised, to be always discreet and silent, won't your more active mates capture the light, obtain satisfaction and leave you only with what no other girl wants? If you don't complain when things go wrong, if you allow people to disrespect you without showing them that you are somebody, how can you bring those who have wronged you to make things right afterwards, the voice would continue. Enotse would immediately put a stop to the small voice. Essentially, to my mind, life is what happens to you when you are busy trying to learn how to live better, she would say to herself. This means that every minute of your life is important because every minute you live gives you information about yourself and the environment in which you are trying to live and grow up, she would muse. Even the difficulties you face now and then are important because they test your faith in your capacity to move on and go ahead with living, she would continue to argue with herself. The fact that a hen has broken legs does not stop it from searching for worms. She saw life as a succession of sunlight and darkness, a succession of rainy season and dry season. During trying periods, or when things did not go on as planned, one needed to be patient because tomorrow always brought newer and often better tidings and promises. Rather than spend her time complaining or being envious of other women, she therefore lived the moment, the present, the now, because she felt that there was no need waiting to become toothless before trying to relish the bony wings of the chicken. Each day spent complaining was to her wasted, the joys it could bring not properly identified because of a blindness that seemed to affect those who were bent on seeing what went wrong rather than what did not go wrong. She vowed to always force herself to see what went according to one's wishes and to partake of the tranquillity of spirit that this inevitably generated. For her, this was the only intelligent method of accepting life.

Enotse was learning how to knit and sew dresses with some of her age mates in a shed owned by an Ibo family. She was about fourteen years old. A few weeks earlier, her age mates had celebrated the wedding of one of them who had been given as a second wife to a very influential businessman in the village called Isaac Oja. Isaac Oja was about the richest man in the village. He was the only one who had a Honda motorcycle, in addition to having two Raleigh bicycles. People knew from afar when he was leaving his house for his store in the village because each time, he would start his motorcycle and rev the engine as loud as possible. He would then blow the horn every minute even when there was no obstacle on the way to his store. Children would run after him, shouting excitedly, some trying unsuccessfully to outrun the motorcycle. His house was the only house in the village with roofs in corrugated iron sheets and coloured windows. His children had all gone to Okrumi. Okrumi was the name the villagers gave to the Nigerian capital city, Lagos. Those who went to Okrumi always came back with a transistor radio and a harmonica. They would tune in to stations that played juju and high life music and would turn the volume up loudly so that others around them could listen and imagine how exciting life in the city was. Then they would bring out their shining harmonicas and with their mouths produce different melodies which they named with very nice-sounding and intelligent titles. Many teenage girls dreamt of getting married to Isaac Oja because they imagined he would take them with him one day to Okrumi. The news people heard was that the journey there lasted several days but that it was worth the trouble because life in Okrumi was the most exciting one could have. There was no need to go to the river because in each house, you only needed to turn on a knob for clear water to fill your bucket. There was no need to add kerosene to your bush lamp because all the houses had free electricity. There was no need to walk to where you wanted to go because there were motorcycles, cars, lorries and buses everywhere. Okrumi was thus paradise on earth.

"Isaac Oja's first son is going back to Okrumi soon?"

"So, I've been told. I think I saw him smoking a cigarette yesterday behind his father's house."

"Chei! How can someone sensible do something like that? I'm sure his father doesn't know. This is what happens when you have easy money."

"I'm told he has stopped going to school."

"Does he really need to go to school? His father is strong enough to give him a job with government. The assistant District Officer is the child of one of the richest men in the village where government has built its offices. He never finished his school and see how powerful he is today."

The discussion between Comfort and her age mates was becoming more and more animated. Then one of them spoke about the handsome young man that had translated Father Patrick during his first visit. He had finished his secondary school in Utonkon and had become the headmaster of the only primary school that had been built in the village, St Patrick's Primary School.

"Did you see the way he looked at you the other day?" one of them asked Enotse.

"Oh, please stop talking jazz. How do you want him to look at me when I have never been to school," Enotse replied.

"It is not school that builds character or that makes a good wife," another declared.

"Maybe you are right but going to school makes you better and so you become a better wife, don't you think?" Enotse asked.

"Are you talking of Oyiboman school?" one of them questioned.

"Yes," replied Enotse.

"Do you think Oyiboman school is a place for girls to go? Do they teach you there how to be a good mother? Do they teach you there how to take care of your family? Do they teach you there how to make good bitter leaf soup? Do they teach you there how to know when the yam is cooked well enough to be pounded? What does Oyiboman know about our village? Did our mothers and grandmothers not bring us up very well?

Did they wait to go to Oyiboman school to learn how not to put too much salt or too much pepper in the soup?" the same girl wondered.

"I agree with you, but I still think that going to school is very useful. When you learn Oyiboman language and culture, you know more things. When you know more things, you are able to say what is right and what is wrong. When you are able to see and say what is right and what is wrong, you can guide those around you, including members of your family," Enotse affirmed.

"Maybe you're right, my sister. But it is not Oyiboman language or culture that will give me a husband or tell me when to plant my cassava or teach me how to plait the hair of my daughter," yet another girl declared.

"There are things our fathers and mothers know, and they teach them to us. But there are other things they don't know. These are what Oyiboman schools are created for. With what you learn from there, you can listen to and understand the radio for example. You can go to Okrumi and live there with no wahala at all. You can talk with people who do not speak our mother tongue," said one of them who agreed with Enotse's point of view.

"Okrumi is not where I want to live, no way!" someone added vehemently

"Why?" requested one of them.

"I hear that policeman there is free to catch you when he wants," was answered.

"Is that so?" Enotse asked.

"Yes, they walk around with koboko and when you resist arrest, they flog you until you start to bleed well well," one of the girls announced with authority.

"They arrest you only if you do bad things, no be so?" another asked quizzically.

"No, I hear that Okrumi is a police state and that you must give dash to policeman if you want to live without harassment," the girl who made the announcement said, with authority.

"If Okrumi is a police state, why are many people rushing to live there?" Enotse asked with incredulity.

"The people who go to live there are either rich, like Oja, or they have lots of juju, which protects them from the police," responded the girl who had made the announcement.

"I hear that there are many young girls who work in Okrumi and get rich quickly. Many are able to send money back home to their papa and mama and even build houses with corrugated iron sheet," another girl announced, equally sure of her source of information.

"What kind of work can they do when they have not gone to Oyiboman school? Government work is not for everybody," Enotse wondered.

"No kind of work can replace a husband. I prefer to stay here, marry a man who can look after me well well, have plenty pickins and thank God for his blessings," said the girl who had earlier on agreed with Enotse's point of view.

"My daughter, come and greet your in-laws," Agbo Ochoga ordered one evening when Enotse came back from the river. He was in the shed outside his hut and was with three men who were sitting in a semi-circle facing him. There was a very big keg of palm wine and a calabash bowl that contained white and red kola nuts on a mat in front of him. These had been brought by the visitors. One of the visitors was a member of the Council of Chiefs, the Otse Arekwu, responsible for the masquerades and therefore feared by many because it was known he could converse directly with all the spirits, good or evil, and that he communicated regularly with departed village ancestors. Enotse knelt down to greet him first, before kneeling down in front of the other men to greet them as well. The Otse Arekwu had come on behalf of his son, Peter, the boy who had translated the reverend father's speech and who was now the Headmaster of Saint Patrick Primary School in the village. The Otse Arekwu was with two of his brothers to see Agbo Ochoga, with whom he sat in the Council of Chiefs. He had come to ask that both families be united and that Enotse's father accept her marriage with his son, Teacher. The visitors had not come empty handed. In addition to the palm wine and the kola nuts, they had come with several yards of imported lace material and very expensive Akwete clothes imported from Ghana. They had also come with ten goats and several crates of Coca Cola. It was their first visit and they visibly wanted to impress their prospective future in-laws. Agbo Ochoga was very happy that Teacher, as the respected village headmaster was commonly referred to, had chosen his daughter to become his wife. The dowry was fixed and the union between the two families agreed upon.

The day Enotse left her parents' compound to join her husband's was very joyful. The sky was cloudless and blue and the temperature slightly warm. Her parents' compound was full of activity and excitement. The chief village drummer had been paid to produce first in her father's compound. He had come with three Conga drums and he treated the very large crowd of spectators that had gathered to a rich variety of music, his hands moving from one drum to the other in an order he mastered excellently. Enotse was required to dance and to change her clothes as many times as possible to show that she was from a wealthy family and was moving into another equally wealthy family. Each time she changed, the drummer produced a new tone of music which those who had been initiated translated to others by saying that each in reality told the story of a very happy and united family. All the members of her age grade, the Ayi Ochiba, gathered around her and sang lots of songs praising her parents for having brought her up to become a good wife and praising her in-law's family for making a very good choice. They sang the following songs many times:

The mother of her father
Look at how beautiful she is
The Queen of the compound
Look at how well she dances
Her flat stomach
Will soon be home to future princes and princesses
Her goodness which knows no bounds
Will be rewarded with a thousand blessings
Her home will know no want
We the Ayi Ochiba
Rejoice that one of us will be in Teacher's compound
And will wait patiently
For tomorrow
No bitterness shall be allowed to grow
No shame on her compound but great pride shall rule
No despair but hope
No diseases and suffering but excellent health
Respect for her husband she will not fail
As the new family will in happiness grow and grow and grow

Then the group proceeded to walk from Enotse's father's compound to her future husband's. Along the way, the drummer continued to produce, using different tempos and the Ayi Ochibas matched these with corresponding songs. Enotse was required to dance all the way but most of the time, some of her age mates danced with her. Sometimes, someone from the crowd that was following would stop the procession and start pasting wads of banknotes on the bride's face. The crowd would cheer and the more banknotes were pasted on Enotse's face, the louder the cheer became. Enotse was very happy.

3

"The mistress of the house, where did this illness come from?"

"Illnesses come and go. There is no reason that yours will not finally decide to go, given all the quinine and Panadol your son is asking you to take. Why have you decided not to take them?"

"The juju from the village is more powerful than the quinine tablets. I think I know who does not want me to do my job as village head."

"We should not always be looking for the problem outside the house. The man who asks others to clean his compound but urinates inside his bedroom should not complain of having too many flies on his bed."

"I'm still wondering why she has not called."

"It is not the wondering that will heal you. It is the medicine your son is trying to make you take. It is the food I prepare for you to eat. If you spend all your time worrying, I'm not sure you will get better."

"Chei. How can one be so insensitive and foolhardy? Where did I go wrong?"

"Now is not the time to think. It is the time to do. It is the time to take your tablets and then eat. You will think better when your stomach is full."

"Where did I go wrong?"

4

Her first child was a son, who was named after her father-in-law. Her second was a son, who was named after her paternal grandfather. Her third was a son who was named after one of her brothers-in-law. It was at the birth of her fourth son that she started to smell trouble in the home. Apparently, her husband had been secretly looking forward to having a daughter. He had expected their third and fourth children to be girls and had visibly been very displeased at not having had one. He thought his wife had a problem and told her to go and consult the village seer to find out what the matter was and what solutions needed to be administered.

The seer was respected but especially feared by all in the village. He lived alone and had never been married. His home was about one and a half kilometres away from the village, close to the river that served as a source of water to everyone. His compound faced the dense forest from where the most revered masquerades of the village came out in procession when an elderly man died and had to be buried with due respect. The path leading to this compound was very narrow. It went through a patch of thorny bush which led to a cassava farm that hid the seer's compound from public gaze. There was a long trail of smoke rising into the air above the compound, proof that someone was at home. He was known to eat dog meat. Each time he killed a dog, which he would first tie to a tree, those passing by on their way to the river or to their farms were aware, because each dog would wail for a long time, as the seer used a heavy log of wood to reduce it to silence. The compound was fenced with dried branches of palm tree. At the entrance, there was a mat on the ground on which the dried bodies of several animals, including snakes, lizards and scorpions, were arranged randomly. The compound consisted of a big shed close to the entrance, three huts, and a large barn. The barn was home to a variety of animals including goats, cocks, hens, ducks and dogs.

The seer was eating roasted cocoyam with palm oil when Enotse announced her arrival at the entrance to his compound. She had been told to take six red kola nuts, two hens and one goat to him if she wanted him to be able to correctly read her situation. He gazed at her intently for a few seconds, went inside one of the huts, brought out a small stool, and told Enotse to sit down in the shed. Then he took out his snuff box and examined its contents silently. He grunted and with his right-hand thumb took out of the box some brownish looking powder, which he put into each of his nostrils. Then he sneezed loudly before spitting on the bare floor, swearing all the time. He asked Enotse for one of the red kola nuts she had brought with her. He broke this into three parts, each time mumbling things that were unintelligible to Enotse. Then he told her to hand over one of the hens she had brought. He took out a knife and with a swift movement cut the hen's throat. He allowed the hen's blood to spill into a circle that he had drawn with a piece of white chalk on the bare brown floor. He saw the way the blood was dripping from the hen and he seemed satisfied. He waited until the blood had finished dripping. He then closed his eyes for a few minutes, all the while singing silently to himself. When he finally opened his eyes, he gazed at

Enotse but had a faraway look and something that seemed like a smile seemed to form around his lips. He dipped his hands into a raffia basket that contained lots of black and white beads. Without counting the beads, he threw what he had gathered up into the air and allowed them to drop on the floor, next to the circle he had drawn earlier, with patches of blood here and there. He had taken seven beads, three white and four black beads. He read their respective positions and nodded his head in satisfaction. He then collected the beads one after the other and threw each up twice before reading their individual messages. He nodded his head in satisfaction each time. Afterwards, he took one piece of the kola nut which he had broken earlier and broke it into smaller pieces. He mumbled some words, offered them to his departed ancestors, thanking them for giving him the wisdom to read the problem that was at hand today. Next, he grabbed a bottle of local gin which he had placed under his chair, took a mouthful which he immediately gulped down, and turned to look at Enotse with bloodshot eyes.

"You will have many children. They will grow and take care of you. You will have a daughter."

Enotse had twin sons during her following pregnancy. It was a very difficult pregnancy and one of the twins was terribly ill at birth. He never stopped crying and vomiting and trembling. Her husband became less and less patient with her and would get angry for no visible reason. He thought Enotse was cursed and that this was why she could not give birth to daughters. He started spending less time at home and coming home late. In reality, he had started looking for a second wife, which he felt was becoming of his position as a village notable.

Enotse's father-in-law frowned at the behaviour of his

son.

"Teacher, do you know what you're doing?"

"Yes, Father."

"Are you sure? No sensible man with a wife and children at home forgets his responsibilities."

"I'm not forgetting my responsibilities, Father. It is not me who has problems."

"Who has?"

"I'm sure you know."

"You come home very late every night and you're telling me you don't have a problem, is that so?"

"Father, all my age mates have big families. Why should I not have one myself?"

"Nothing is stopping you from having a big family. That should not be a reason for you to neglect what you have already. Don't forget that while you're wasting your time fighting to dress the hens outside the house, the dog is defecating in your parlour. The dog remains with the master who treats him well."

"I hear what you are saying, Father. But I want to be like my age mates, have two or three wives, have lots of children, and especially daughters."

"Is that so? You want to be like your age mates! You want to have two or three wives! You are not satisfied with the one you have. Do you know that the dog has only one tongue with which he cleans himself? That you wish to have a second wife does not mean you should not take care of the first."

"I have not abandoned her."

"You have not abandoned her! You spend the whole time in someone else's compound until the firewood used to cook the evening meal has gone very cold, come back to your compound when no responsible man is roaming the street and you are telling me you have not abandoned her? Even when you're very hungry, you do not touch the plate reserved for your mother-in-law. There are things we avoid doing out of respect for the other."

"I want to have a daughter."

"Who tells you that you won't have one?"

"I have been waiting for too long."

"Who tells you another wife would give you daughters? There are many of your age mates who would like to have sons like you do have, who have none for the moment, but who are behaving responsibly, like men."

"I want to have a daughter."

"We should be proud of our children, no matter their sex. The hand is useless without the fingers. A good father does not count the number of children he has nor does he select who among these he prefers. A good father is a father, full stop."

"I have not said that I am not grateful for having the children I have. They are all doing very well at school. But I want to also have daughters, to have the joy of girls singing in my compound."

"We do not choose the children we have. It is God's choice. There are many fathers who have only girls in their compound. I have not heard them complaining and wailing and asking the gods of Agila to justify their choice."

"I am not asking the gods of Agila to justify their choice. Having children is not the choice of God or of gods but mine, and mine alone. If I want to have a daughter, I will do what I can to have one."

Teacher thought his wife had a problem and started spending much of his time in the evenings in a neighbouring compound, the Obande's. He was not the only one spending his evenings there. There were usually three or four men, some of them already married, who tried to impress Obande and his second wife, both father and mother to Orinya, a very beautiful young girl. Orinya seemed to make all the men in the village lose their senses. She had a carefree attitude and a way of walking that seemed to make her the centre of attraction anywhere she went. Her hair was always plaited as if she had a pyramid on her head. When she walked across different squares in the village, conversations between men who usually gathered there to chat stopped as each one admired the pointed nipples under construction. Orinya was very much aware of the effect she had on the menfolk. When she danced with her young age mates, it was customary for each one of them to dance solo for a while to the cheers of spectators. Orinya always waited to be the last to dance and she had a particular way of twisting her buttocks that sent most of the men screaming. Then she would smile. She had the whitest set of teeth in the village and people wondered what type of chewing stick she used. Her smile added to her beauty and many of the young men around dreamt of being the lucky winner of such a trophy. It was therefore only natural for her parents' compound to attract different potential suitors from all over the village.

Orinya's father wanted his daughter to marry a man who could facilitate her access to Western education or at least help improve her social situation. Teacher, being the village headmaster seemed to fit perfectly such a profile. He was warmly welcomed each time he went visiting, which was every day. He would buy a keg of palm wine each time he went and would spend the time telling them news about Nigeria, news he had learnt from the radio. He told those who sometimes gathered around him that trouble was brewing in the Western Region where many factions were engaged in a do-or-die battle to control the organs of government. He seemed to enjoy being the focus of attention, seemed to like how those around him listened to him open-mouthed. He also seemed very happy that he had been chosen among the list of suitors as Obande's future son-in-law. The fact that Orinya would be a second wife was accepted as a good sign by her father, who knew that Enotse would treat her not as an opponent but as her child.

Teacher began complaining about lots of things in his home. He started getting very easily irritated about things he thought Enotse was doing or had done wrongly in his home. He would complain that there was not enough meat in the egusi soup or that the plate of garri was not hot enough. The beatings started one evening when the ill twin refused to eat and spent long hours crying.

"What kind of woman is this who allows her child to cry until he has no more tears?" he thundered.

"You know he is ill and has been ill since he was born. His face is hot, and his body is sweating. Everything he eats comes out immediately. There is blood in his excrement. I have given him the potion I made with the dried bark of the village iroko tree, but nothing has changed," Enotse answered.

"A normal woman and mother ties a sick child to her back, rather than abandon the child on the cold mat on the ground," he said angrily.

"What we need to do is to take him to the general hospital at Nkalagu. The illness he has is too serious for the village herbalist to heal. I asked you last week to give me some money so that I can hire a bicycle to go there. I am still waiting for your answer."

"What your son has is called dysentery," he finally declared.

"If you know what he has, why did you not tell me this earlier than now? And if you know what he has, why have you not found the solution? Maybe you do not have the time."

Enotse tried all she could to calm the ill child down to no avail. Suddenly, her husband hit her violently on the face. Her upper lip was cut and drops of blood started to fall on the ground. The sight of blood had no effect on her husband, who continued slapping, boxing and kicking her. The ill son and other children in the compound only cried louder. This attracted the attention of immediate neighbours who arrived and stood between husband and wife. One of the men present held Teacher's hand, told him not to be angry anymore and advised that the family as well as the entire compound be allowed to now sleep peacefully. "Hot water inevitably becomes cold with time," he added.

"When do you think I will be able to have a complete family?" Teacher asked.

"She is still a child," Obande answered.

"She is a child woman, because she has reached the age of bearing children," Teacher continued.

"What is important is not to bear children but to rear them."

"She won't be alone in rearing them."

"That is true. I know Enotse's value and I know Orinya can count on her. But I still think she's a child. There are things she needs to learn herself, first. You do not teach anybody how to taste something that is sweet."

"I agree. You know water is cold only after you have

touched it. But Orinya can learn things for herself under my roof and in my compound."

"I am not sure she's ripe yet. You give a hoe to someone who you know can use it."

"I'm sure you have brought Orinya up extremely well."

"Try to be patient. There is always daybreak after a night, no matter how long the night lasts."

The health of Enotse's son continued to deteriorate. She multiplied her visits to the village herbalist who gave her a variety of solutions including an ointment which she was supposed to rub on his body every hour and a drink made from the leaves of a medicinal tree which the herbalist was the only one capable of preparing. This did not stop her son's body from burning like hot charcoal. He was always vomiting and crying and this seemed to infuriate her husband all the more.

"We have to take him to Nkalagu. I hope it is not too late."

Her husband pretended not to have heard her.

"Oga, I'm begging you to listen to me. We have to go to Nkalagu. Either you take us there on your bicycle or you give me money to hire someone to take us there, please."

"If you want to go to Nkalagu, that is your problem. It is your wickedness that is being punished by the gods."

"It is not because the tooth is sharp that it willingly bites the tongue. The gods who gave me a child will give me the strength to mother him well."

Enotse finally got someone to take her to the hospital three days afterwards. They had to leave the village very early in the morning, well before the cocks started to crow because the journey was going to be long. She tied her son to her back and sat on the rear seat of the bicycle. When the rider first took off, the bicycle was not stable at all and crashed, sending rider and passengers to the ground. They got up and tried taking off a second time and crashed again, ending up in the grass along the path. The ill child was quiet all the while. At the third trial, the rider was able to stabilize the bicycle and the journey finally began.

Hardly had they left the village than the ill son began crying loudly. Enotse suddenly felt some warm liquid wetting her back. She tried to calm her son down by singing the following song:

Bomboy, why are you crying?
The pain you have
Share it with me
I know you are suffering
But extreme suffering is not death
When you withstand such suffering
This shows you are alive
You will live to laugh at this day
Because soon you'll be well and running around the house
With your brothers and cousins
Soon you'll be asking for more akara
To quench your hunger
Don't cry anymore my son
The Nkalagu doctor will heal you before night falls today
Don't cry anymore my father
Please, don't cry anymore

It was the first time Enotse had left the village. It was the first time she was in a big city. What struck her first was the noise. There was loud music coming from several shops owned by Ibo traders who seemed to be engaged in a competition for which shop could drown the others, volume wise. There were taxis blowing their horns regularly to attract the attention of potential passengers. There were motorcycles of different sizes and colours. Nkalagu was an extremely busy city. A very large cement factory was located there. The hospital was located in the GRA or Government Residential Area. This was a zone of the city with official houses built and reserved for senior government civil servants. Each house had its boys' quarter reserved for the house boy or house girl employed by each civil servant. Each quarter contained two bedrooms, a living room, a kitchen, a bathroom and a toilet. The houses and their boys' quarters were all painted in white with the exception of the windows which were in black. Around each house, Enotse saw lots of flowerbeds filled with flowers of different colours. Unlike the city centre, which was full of noise, the GRA was quiet and calm. The streets were lined with different types of trees which provided a welcome shade that protected the dozens and dozens of pedestrians and cyclists who were either going to or coming from the hospital. The shade provided temporary solace to Enotse, who asked the bicycle rider to please go faster.

The hospital was big. There was a single gate which served both as an entrance and an exit. Motor bikes and cars were blowing their horns while cycles were ringing their bells to clear their path. Many vendors selling different types of food, newspapers, cigarettes, towels, handkerchiefs, cheap sunglasses and various sorts of objects were loudly advertising their wares and inviting potential customers not to lose the opportunity of making a good bargain. The first port of call was the registration office where Enotse was required to pay for an admission card. Enotse asked the clerk what an admission card meant and she was told it was a card she would need to present to the doctor when it would be her turn to see him.

"How much is the card?" Enotse asked very politely.

"It is only one pound," the clerk answered impatiently.

"One pound, that is quite expensive," Enotse commented.

"Old woman, there are many people waiting on the line behind you, so please don't waste my time," the man retorted angrily.

"Please don't be angry," Enotse begged.

Fortunately, she had brought some money with her, so she paid for the card. Then they were told to proceed to a large waiting room which was already crowded with people. Children were crying, elderly people were groaning, and a nurse was shouting at someone who did not seem to understand the instructions she had given. It was extremely hot and humid and the ceiling fan in the waiting room wasn't working. The heat in the room was unbearable but there was no other place to go to while waiting for the doctor, so Enotse remained in the room. She gave the rider who had accompanied her some money to go and buy some food from one of the women who were selling cooked rice and beans at the entrance to the hospital. She asked him to buy some bananas and oranges for her.

Enotse was told she would have to spend the night at Nkalagu hospital. She was told the doctors had more urgent things to do and that he would be free to handle her case only the following morning. Her son passed away that night. Enotse knew he had gone because he had not cried for several hours. A night nurse confirmed her son's death. Enotse felt there was no need waiting for the doctor anymore, so she decided that they needed to ride back to the village. There was moonlight so the path they had taken when they rode to Nkalagu would be visible. She tied the corpse of her child to her back and they proceeded out of the hospital.

They cut a few fresh branches of palm tree which they tied to the front and back of the bicycle. It was believed that the green leaves of palm trees gave solace to the departed and so made the transportation of their dead bodies much easier. There was a story told of a Christian family who did not believe in such superstition, and who decided to transport the body of an old member of their family from a city fifty miles away from the village without the leaves of a palm tree. The vehicle in which the corpse was being transported started to zigzag uncontrollably along the road until the driver got the message and stopped to attach fresh branches of a palm tree to the bonnet of his vehicle before driving safely afterwards to the village.

The moonlight was suddenly covered by black clouds. Several owls could be heard hooting nearby. One of them emitted a high-pitched shriek, that made the bicycle rider stop in his tracks.

"This baby is strong," announced the bicycle rider.

"What do you mean?" asked the mother.

"I cannot control the bicycle. When I try to avoid holes on the path, a strong force pushes the bicycle right into the hole. There is a strong wind that is slowing me down," he explained.

"Yes, I can feel the wind," she acknowledged.

"Can you see the sky? It has suddenly become very dark," he warned.

"I can hear thunder from afar. I see some lightning just above our heads. I smell rain in the air," she observed.

"How can a young spirit who has not lived have so much power of revenge?" the rider wondered.

The sky was now totally black. Occasionally, lightning struck and temporarily illuminated the path along which the rider was struggling to advance. An animal scuttled right in front of the bicycle. The rider tried to avoid it, was unable to control his bicycle, and crashed into a big tree in the nearby bush. A family of bats flew out of the tree, squeaking noisily, apparently angry at having had their resort invaded. The hooting of the owls continued, unabated. Then the sky suddenly opened, and the rain started falling in heavy large drops. The path became slippery. The rain, the thunderstorm, the lightning and the strong wind made it impossible to continue riding. Suddenly, the rain stopped, and the lightning disappeared. The night was once again plunged into total darkness. The bicycle rider could no longer see the path on which to ride. He did not move. Enotse prayed loudly, asking her departed son not to be angry and wishing him safe journey for his very short trip to wherever he was going. A few minutes later, a swarm of fireflies appeared, seemingly inviting Enotse and the bicycle rider to follow them, but on foot. The journey to the village was finished on foot.

They got back to the village very early in the morning. A group of women who had woken up early and were preparing to go to the farm saw the wet green leaves on the bicycle and started wailing. Two of them approached Enotse, unwrapped the wet body from her back and placed it on a mat, while they continued to weep profusely. Another went into her hut and brought a wooden bench for Enotse to sit on. A third offered the bicycle rider a bowl of water to drink. The crying attracted neighbours. When they saw the bundle on the mat, everyone started wailing. Enotse's husband was not at home. Nobody knew where he had gone to. One of the elders in the compound asked two teenage boys to start digging a grave behind one of the houses. The dead boy's body was then wrapped in one of his mother's colourful clothes and quickly buried. Teacher arrived later in the morning, told the women who had stayed to assist his wife to stop crying and to go back to their homes and prepare to go to their farms. Orinya joined his household the following day as his second wife.

"Greetings to the mother of the house." Enotse heard someone say. She went out and saw one of her younger brothers who was on his way to the farm.

"Greetings to you too," she replied.

"How is your body?" he went on to ask.

"We thank God," she answered.

"And your second, are you doing well?"

"Why should we quarrel?" Enotse asked. "She is younger than my second son. Can you see me quarrelling with someone who I saw naked for a long time?"

"Does she go to the farm?"

"Not at all. My husband says she doesn't need to go to the farm. She spends her day plaiting and braiding her hair and waiting for him to come back from school. It is none of my business as long as my children have enough to eat every day."

"Does she show you respect?"

"Yes of course. When she sees me trying to pound yams in the mortar, she immediately comes to help me. She goes to the river to fetch water for the household. Yes, she shows me respect. My problem is not with her but with my husband."

"You shouldn't worry too much. Even though the man brings prosperity to the home, it is the woman who remains the mistress. You are the headmistress and no matter what he does with other women and how much time he spends with them, it is to you he'll turn when the going gets tough."

"The problem is that he has not given me any money to buy foodstuff for the family for a very long time."

"Is that so?"

"Yes. Fortunately, I sell garri in the market and the small profit I make enables me to feed everyone."

"Do you want me to have a talk with him?"

"No, you shouldn't. You know how very easily he gets angry. When he gets angry, he lashes out at anyone close by. No, don't bother talking to him. As long as my children have enough to eat, I can manage."

"How are they doing at school?"

"I think they are all doing fine. Since their father is the headmaster, he is there to take care of them, abi?"

"Yes of course. Let me be off to the farm. The bird that spends the whole day singing will not have anything to eat. Greet your husband for me."

"OK, he will hear. Beware of poisonous snakes."

"Don't worry. If you don't step on a snake, it doesn't bite you. Goodbye."

"Go well."

Orinya's first child was a girl. Teacher was so elated that he celebrated this birth by killing a cow. The girl was named Enotse, after the first wife. Then came the second child, equally a girl. Teacher killed a cow for the second time.

"Teacher, do you know what you're doing?" Teacher's father enquired one day, with apprehension.

"Why are you asking Father?" Teacher responded, politely.

"You must be happy that you have started having the big family you have been craving for," his father went on.

"Yes, Father. I'm very happy," Teacher replied, all smiles.

"Do you hear what people are saying?" his father asked, sternly.

"No, not at all," Teacher answered, meekly.

"The person who wants to produce charcoal is not afraid of smoke. The person who sweats is sure not to go empty-handed," his father lectured.

"I promised her father that she would not do any farming," Teacher answered with discomfort.

"The cat that you feed regularly every day allows rats to invade your home," his father continued his lecture.

"I promised her father she would not break her back under the sun," Teacher repeated.

"It is with the water that comes out of your body that you are able to draw water from the well. You do not go to take honey from the beehive if you do not accept to be stung by bees," his father added.

"I will find something for her to do, don't worry Father," Teacher promised.

"A hen eats the worm only after it has uncovered it by tilling the earth," his father continued, unconvinced by Teacher's explanations.

"I will find something for her to do, soon. For the meantime, I can provide for her," Teacher announced proudly.

"Beauty does not fill the basket with yams or produce the spinach and smoked fish needed to prepare soup for the family," his father concluded gravely.

Orinya, now referred to as Mama Baby, was still not going to work in the farm nor did she go to sell things in the market.

She would spend the whole day plaiting her daughters' hair and waiting for her husband to come back from school. When he came back, he was presented with two trays containing meals, prepared by his two wives. He would complain that there weren't many pieces of meat in the soup prepared by his first wife. He usually ate nothing prepared by her. One day she found the courage to tell him that there would be meat in what she prepared if he gave her money to buy some in the market. He got very angry and beat her severely. She was unable to go to the market for several days to sell her wares. She could not however stay indoors all the time because there were lots of things to do in the home. This was because in addition to her children, Enotse, as the first wife and so headmistress of the home, had four young brothers-in-law in the house to take care of. This meant preparing meals almost all the time. Preparing meals meant having to go to the bush regularly to cut some firewood and to the river to fetch some water. She organised herself in such a way that she had the time to do these chores when her children had gone to school in the morning. Her regular customers who wanted to buy garri from her and knew she was unable to be at her shed in the market came to see her at home. She therefore had enough money to buy such necessary ingredients like salt, palm oil, tomatoes and onions to prepare various types of stew and soup.

She tried to prepare the soup which her husband liked the most, egusi soup. This was made with melon seeds that were ground. The ground seeds were then put into boiling water with smoked fish and ground crayfish. Afterwards, some drops of palm oil and several bitter leaves were added. This usually produced a sweet bitter flavour she knew her husband appreciated. She gave some money to one of the children after they had come back from school and sent him to go to the market and buy several smoked fish and several packets of ground crayfish. One of her brothers-in-law told her his mouth was already watering. When she retrieved her tray from her husband, the soup was cold and untouched.

Sometimes, some of the schoolteachers came to see Teacher at home after school. Many spoke to him with deference as if he was God. One was an exception. People called him Heleber. He was quite intelligent and extremely funny. He was called Heleber because he always used the word 'Heleber' in his sentences when he became excited or when he wanted to speak seriously:

"I can't go to heleber now because when I heleber, I get quite tired."

"Why should I heleber? Absolute rubbish! It is my choice to heleber or not to heleber, okay?"

"If government continues to heleber for a long time, we will all heleber and that will be the end of the heleber."

"The other day, I went to a festival to heleber and just as I was about to heleber, I changed my mind and decided to do something else."

One day, Heleber came to visit Teacher. He called one of Enotse's sons who had a very protruding big stomach.

"What did you learn at school today?"

"The multiplication table of three."

"So, what is three times ten?"

"Three times ten is thirty, sir."

"Are you sure?"

"Yes, sir."

"Have you learnt the months of the year."

"Yes, sir."

"Can you then tell me how many days have all the months of the year?"

"Yes, sir. Thirty days has September, April, June and November. All the rest have thirty-one days except February alone which has but twenty-eight days in a normal year and twenty-nine days in a leap year."

"Excellent! You are extremely intelligent. Is it your mother you have followed or your father?"

"I don't know, sir."

"I'm sure it's your mother."

"I don't know, sir."

"What do you want to do when you become old."

"Teacher, sir."

"Is that so? So next time you'll be asking me to recite multiplication tables and if I don't know them, you'll flog me, abi?"

"No, sir."

"Aha, so if you become a teacher, you'll never flog your pupils?"

"No, sir."

"When they don't know the answer, what will you do?"

"I don't know, sir."

"When they forget their homework at home will you punish them?"

"No, sir."

"If you don't punish them, how will they know they are not doing things right?"

"I don't know, sir."

"Wonderful. Do you fight at school?"

"No, sir."

"When others come to look for your trouble, what do you

do?"

"Nothing, sir."

"Erm, what did you eat today that your belly is full like this?"

"I don't remember, sir."

"Is it jollof rice or akamu?"

"I don't remember, sir."

"Did you leave any for me?"

"No, sir."

"Wonderful! So, you ate everything fiam fiam without leaving anything behind. Heleber!"

"I don't know, sir."

"Next time you must leave something for me, okay?"

"Yes, sir."

"The head of the fowl and the legs and the wings."

"Yes, sir."

"You're a very good boy. Take this one penny and go and buy some sweets."

"Thank you, sir."

Heleber then went to speak to Teacher with a very worried tone.

"I hear that Major Kaduna has struck and that the Sardauna has been killed."

"I'm not sure the Northerners will take his death kindly. He is not the only one who has been killed. Balewa is reported to have been killed too."

"This is going to be a big heleber. Do you think Ironsi has the force to keep things under control?"

"Is he not a military man? Are they not taught how to maintain order and discipline?"

"Yes, but this time the disorder is within the military.

There is going to be a big heleber, I repeat."

"Let's wait and see."

Heleber came back a few days later, looking extremely worried.

"The big heleber has started. Ironsi and many others around him have been killed. The heleber that has started will turn into Armageddon if care is not taken."

"I think Ironsi dug his own grave. You do not try to create a united country by military fiat without taking into account its diversity. You do not surround yourself only with Ibo advisers when the Hausas are weeping for their lost dignitaries."

"Yes, but where will an eye-for-an-eye solution lead us all? Heleber, my God!"

Heleber came back sometime afterwards looking aghast and extremely anxious. He engaged a discussion with Teacher.

"If Odumegwu Ojukwu decides to heleber, there is no way we can avoid a civil war," he said.

"I do not think Yakubu Gowon will accept or tolerate Ojukwu's manners," Teacher replied. "Don't forget that his name stands for Go On With One Nigeria."

"If Ojukwu decides to heleber, and war is declared against the Ibos, Agila will heleber because the Ibos have been our neighbours since time immemorial."

"That is true. Our people and the Ibos have a long history of living together. When we are ill, it is to Nkalagu we go to be healed. Our village is surrounded by many Ibo villages. War should be avoided but I'm not sure if it is not too late," Teacher continued.

"The school will have to heleber, won't it?"

"Eventually, yes, but we should pray war is not declared."

"I'm told Ojukwu has already had the heleber of a number

of foreign European powers and several West African Presidents like the President of Ivory Coast. This will surely make him more determined to create his independent Biafra."

"You are right, but a greater number of foreign and West African governments are in favour of Yakubu Gowon."

"I'm also told Ojukwu has bought many jet bombers and has recruited many European pilots all of whom have fought during previous world wars. Lagos will be bombed and destroyed in the twinkle of an eye."

"Where did he get the money from?"

"From Ivory Coast."

"And where are the jet bombers stationed?"

"In a secret heleber close to Enugu airport."

"Let's hope things will work out. We are brothers with the Ibos, and it is normal for us to quarrel once in a while. The calabashes that are tied together are forced to touch and irritate one another. But that should not degenerate into unnecessary violence."

"Yes, I hope things will heleber down because once war starts, no one knows when it will end."

Every evening when he came back from school, Teacher would take out his rosary and spend long hours mumbling things to himself and walking from one end of the compound to the other. Afterwards, he would turn on his transistor radio with a very worried expression on his face. Each time he finished listening to the news, he would have a more worried expression on his face and would resume his mumblings with his rosary. A few days later, Heleber came back to Teacher's compound. Gone was the jovial face.

"Have you heard the heleber news? The headless body of an Agila man was found in his farm close to the border with the Ibo village five miles away."

"The Republic of Biafra was declared recently, and federal troops are preparing to march down to Enugu to show Ojukwu pepper," Teacher answered confidently.

"My problem is not with Enugu but with Agila. We are at war with our neighbours and anything can heleber anytime."

"What arrangements have been made by Ogaba Idu, the village chief?" Teacher asked.

"He has informed the necessary masculine age grades to prepare for war. Some will remain in the village to defend it while others will be asked to go towards some Ibo villages to prevent their men from advancing towards our village," Heleber replied.

"Do you know who has been killed?" Teacher asked.

"No. All I know is that he's from the Ogbilolo lineage. It is normally their turn to produce the next District Head of Agila."

"I see. It must be Agbese, the head of the Agbese family. It was from his compound that we heard gun shots this morning," Teacher concluded.

"Let's go together to his compound to pay our respects. Your first wife must come with us. It is her privilege. She must come and cry with the other women," Heleber suggested.

The more they approached Agbese's compound, the louder the wailing grew. The compound was very big. Agbese had six wives and each wife had two huts, one reserved for their children and the other where they slept and stored their things, including foodstuff. Agbese's own hut was the largest of all and it was built in the centre of the compound. A shed had been prepared in front of this hut and many men sat on long benches that had been arranged inside the shed. Many mats were placed outside the shed for the women to sit on. The convention was that each woman who arrived newly had to cry louder than the others and throw herself on the ground to show the degree of her grief. This lasted a minute or two after which one of the relatives of the deceased would gently pull the woman up from the ground and in a very soothing voice tell her not to be sorrowful anymore because life and death are parts of the same story. Enotse did her crying and expressed her sorrow before sitting down with the other women to weep more silently. The men were engaged in discussing the war effort.

"Our guns are louder. Our bullets are original bullets, made in Europe. They are not second-hand ones made in Onitsha or in Enugu. We will defeat them."

"Yes, our ancestors will not allow them to come within ten miles of our village."

"Yes, no one should go to farm alone anymore. Our women should not go very far into the bush to cut firewood anymore. We are going to place sentries at many strategic points around the village. Agbese's death has to be revenged."

"I'm sure our former friends, the Ibos, know that our anger is very hot. They know we are not cowards. They know they have offended us and that such an offence will not go unpunished."

"Don't you think we should move for peace with them rather than start a war with them?" a voice suggested.

"The war has already started. Agbese's body is here but where is his head? It is the head that is buried and not the legs or the arms. Only the head of our enemy can make Agbese's rest peacefully," another voice explained.

"I hear the war is national and even international. Agila is no longer alone in its fight against the Ibos. I have always found them too proud and even more big-headed than the Oyibos. They believe they own this village. Look at the way the Ibo traders talk to us when we go to their shops to buy batteries for our torch lamp or mosquito coils for the night. Look at the accent they use in their English. They think they are the light of Nigeria. They want to become independent because they think they will have lots of money from the oil that is flowing from Port Harcourt. No, we should stop them in their tracks. And the stopping will begin here in Agila, by the powers of our ancestors," another very vocal voice emphasised.

"What will happen to those that have married Ibo wives?" somebody wondered.

"An Ibo wife married to an Agila man is Agila because her children are Agila," another man replied.

"Can such women be trusted? You should never ask a dog to be the guardian of a plate of meat and bones in your absence," the man who asked the question added.

"The women are all intelligent. They know that you cannot put your hands in the fire and then be surprised to have them burnt," someone else affirmed.

An expedition was sent the following day to a neighbouring Ibo village. It was headed by a very strong, tall and agile young man called Ikor. Ikor was an exceptional hunter. It was rumoured that he needed neither a gun nor a spear to kill the bush meat he always brought home after every hunting expedition. Some people believed he used magic to paralyse the animals which he would then seize with his bare hand before breaking their necks. His hearing was so well developed that he could hear a snake sliding in the grass more than one hundred meters away or the whisper of people hiding in the bush within the same distance. Ikor was also extremely handsome. He was quite young but he already had two wives who seemed to be going along well with one another.

It was towards sunset that the expedition came back. People heard the village drum and went quickly to the market square to see what was happening. In the centre of the square, there was a very giant locust bean tree that was several centuries old. Some of its very large roots were above the ground and these were usually used as seats by traders during market days or by elders during the ujo or new yam festival. Three bodiless heads with glazed eyes and gaping mouths were now arranged below one of these roots. Some men came around to chase all the women and children who were staring silently at these from the vicinity. They argued that war was a matter for men only. Enotse felt sorry for the children of those whose heads were being displayed as trophy. What would happen if my husband went out one day and didn't come back, she fearfully wondered?

The war and enmity between Agila and its Ibo neighbours got more serious with an ever-increasing number of casualties on both sides. The locust bean tree was home to a countless number of bloody heads which were afterwards thrown into a pit at the outskirts of the village. One day, the expedition came back and Ikor was missing. It was a tragedy for the entire village. Then gunshots started being heard much closer to the village. A message of alarm was sent to Otukpo, the district headquarters seventy kilometres away. Ogaba Idu, the village head, implored the relevant authorities there to send in soldiers or policemen to protect the village. A lorry of policemen arrived two days afterwards. The gunshots were now much closer to the village. The policemen went to battle and suffered many casualties. Their commander took the decision to go back to the district headquarters the following morning. Teacher went to discuss with the commander of the police squad for a few hours.

The next morning, he and his family all abandoned the village with the policemen. Two people were invited to sit in the driver's cabin in front of the Bedford lorry which was much more comfortable than the wooden benches at the back. Teacher chose Orinya to sit with him next to the driver all through the journey. It was reported a few days afterwards that the village had been attacked by the Ibos and that people had fled their homes and abandoned everything they possessed. When they returned, they found their huts burnt down, their domestic animals killed and all the shops in the market square looted. During the civil war, which lasted three years, the village was attacked and abandoned this way several times.

While in the village, Teacher had been advised by his father to build a house in Otukpo, the district headquarters, where members of the family could stay, each time they were in the city. He had bought a plot of land and had been able to pay for the building of two small houses facing each other. A well had been dug in-between both houses from which water could be obtained for use in cooking, bathing and washing things. A small bucket was tied to a rope and it was this bucket that was used to fetch water from the well. One of the houses was slightly bigger than the other because it had a bigger living room, two bedrooms and a veranda. The smaller house contained only one room and had no veranda. When the family arrived from the village, Teacher asked his second wife to choose which of the houses she wanted as hers. Enotse found this very strange and told her husband so.

"It is normally the headmistress of the house who should choose first," she said.

"It is the person who builds the house who decides who sleeps where," Teacher replied.

"I hope you know what you're doing," Enotse continued.

"Don't tell me what I should do or not do," he replied.

"You have decided to give pre-eminence to a child and to her children. She has given you soup to drink that has turned your head. I hope you know what you're doing," Enotse repeated.

"If you are not satisfied, you may leave the home," he went on to say.

"Leave the home for a child whom I saw naked at birth to bring up my own children? Tuffia!"

"She is not a child anymore," Teacher argued.

"A woman who stays at home plaiting her head all the time, listening to music on the radio, and gossiping with her age mates instead of going to the market to sell things so that she can buy food for her children is a child for any sensible man to see. You give her money to feed her children but what about me? Are you saying my children are not your children? What have I done that should warrant such a treatment from you?" Enotse asked.

"If you are not satisfied, the door is wide open for you. Anyway, I will be away to the University next month. I need to have a diploma in education in order to start teaching in a secondary school here in the city and join the senior civil service. You will have to look for a way to be financially independent until I come back."

"I have been financially independent for a long time.

When last did you give me something to buy salt for the soup? You think I don't know what is happening in this house? What did you do with all the money you brought from the village? I know you sold all the goats we had in the barn a week before we left."

"Stop asking me questions," he thundered.

Before Enotse said another word, Teacher who could not contain himself anymore, started raining blows on her. Orinya, her housemate, stood apart from the fighting couple, refusing to intervene.

5

"Where did I go wrong? I have tried all my life to bring up my family in peace. I have gone everywhere and travelled long distances so that my family can eat and drink without any difficulty. I have tried to bring light to the village and have not hesitated to contact state and local government officials to ask them not to forget Agila in their development programmes. So why should someone in the village wish me evil."

"Illnesses do not belong only to the poor or to the weak. Even the strongest and the richest fall ill. There is thus no use in asking why one has become ill. One should treat the illness. We are lucky that we have a medical doctor in the family. We should thus follow his advice."

"How come when I follow his advice, take the quinine he has prescribed and eat the food you give me, how come I still vomit everything in my stomach? Eh, can you explain that to me in plain Idoma language?"

"It is not because you sometimes vomit things that you should not follow your son's advice."

"The small chicken does not give lessons to father cock."

"Yes, but the small chicken is what makes father cock and mother hen proud and prosperous."

"I agree that I should consider myself lucky to be in my son's clinic and to be well taken care of. I would surely be better off if I had news from her. Please do not hesitate to wake me up when she calls. I'm sure she soon will."

6

Teacher left Otukpo for the university which was somewhere in the northern parts of the country, in a city called Zaria. He planned to spend only nine months there to obtain a Diploma in Education that would enable him to teach and train teachers. When he arrived in Zaria, he took a taxi to the campus in Samaru, where his studies were being organised. He was given a room in one of the halls of residence, Ribadu Hall, a room he had to share with three other younger students. All three were from rich Hausa families. One possessed a Vespa motorcycle and the two others each had a brand-new Renault 17 TS sports car. Teacher's roommates spent most of the time going to parties. They referred to themselves as "Escape," because they felt that by some stroke of luck, they escaped being constrained to repeat a year, succeeding by miracle in being accepted every year to continue their studies at a higher class. Sometimes when Teacher came back from the Kashim Ibrahim Library late at night, he would find his room filled with a crowd of young boys and girls, drinking, smoking and chatting boisterously. He tried to talk with one of his roommates sometimes afterwards.

"Don't you think you should spend more time with your books and less time with your chicks, as you call them?" he enquired in a paternal tone.

"Are you my old man?" the boy asked angrily.

"I would be worried if I were paying for the university

education of my child who spends his whole day boozing and enjoying life, as you and your friends like to say," he declared.

"Well, you're not my old man in the first place. In the second place, it is not my old man who is footing the bill. It is my state government," the boy proudly explained.

"The fact that you are on state scholarship does not mean you should not do what you are in Zaria for, that is study and obtain a degree," Teacher added, unimpressed.

"I think you're just being envious. You are an old man and you are frustrated. Why not go back to your family and take care of your children? At your age, I surely will not be doing extra hours in the library," the irate boy advised.

"There is no minimum or maximum age for learning. The more you know things, the more you know that there are many things you do not know and that you need to continue learning. It is better to spend hours in the library than while away your energy drinking, dancing and chasing girls at an age when the brain is very fertile," Teacher shot back.

"If you think we are disturbing you, why don't you go to the Chairman of the Hall and ask him to move you to another room?" the boy concluded, furious and walking rapidly away from Teacher.

In addition to the difficulty he had with his roommates, Teacher was facing some serious financial difficulties. He needed not only to buy books but also to feed, at least twice a day. There was a dining hall attached to his hall of residence. Meal tickets were sold at a subsidised price but he neither had a state scholarship nor his salary to be able to buy the standard bundles of thirty or sixty which were sold at the Student Affairs Office. He bought one or two here and there and then finally accepted to turn to his first wife, Enotse, for financial assistance.

Enotse had set up a small retailing shed in front of the family home where she sold lots of things including cassava flour or garri, loaves of bread, and cigarettes. These were things that sold well. Enotse had been able to contact a wholesaler who agreed to supply her with these items and accepted to be paid only after the items had been sold. Her retailing shed soon became a rallying point in the neighbourhood and her commerce started to prosper very well. She was thus able to make enough money to pay for the sustenance of her family as well as help her husband. Her husband told her that what she was giving him to survive in Zaria was a debt he would pay back with interest when he graduated and obtained a better job.

Enotse's children helped her when they came back from school. They would take lots of loaves of bread and cigarettes to a petrol station not very far away from the house where commercial lorries and buses stopped to buy petrol, and would come back with the proceeds of their sale when they finished. Then, things started disappearing from her shed, and sometimes from her house. Someone was stealing things. Enotse would cook some stew with lots of pieces of meat only to find the pot empty of meat the following day. She suspected one of her housemate's children of the thefts but did not know who it was or how he or she was able to organise the thefts. One day, she left her purse containing some money on a stool in her shed for a few minutes because she had to hurry into her room to pick up additional cigarettes to sell. The only children playing around the shed were her stepchildren. When she came back from her room, the purse had disappeared. She asked the children to stop playing and ordered the person who had taken her purse to give it back to her immediately. None of them spoke. Enotse took them one after the other and twisted their ears. They screamed and this attracted the attention of their mother, Orinya, who rushed out and began raining insults on her. Orinya accused Enotse of being a liar, a problem monger, a wicked woman and a frustrated wife. She shouted at her, saying that no one had stolen her purse and that she needed to have her head examined, as their husband often told her.

Things continued to disappear from Enotse's shed. Her husband sent a message that he was staying in Zaria for an additional period. It was then that Enotse decided to buy a big shed in the central city market. She contacted a wholesaler who traded in garri, in rice, in beans and in palm oil and bought the first batch of goods on credit. She was able to pay her rent for the shed, to pay back the wholesaler and began to really make it since she never tired of adding new items to the things she sold. She financed her husband's studies in Zaria, while attending to the needs of all the family in Otukpo, without discrimination. It was at the market that a Yoruba pastor called Pastor Bamidele approached her one day.

"Are you a believer?" he enquired.

"Yes," she answered.

"Praise the Lord! When was the last time you went to church?" he pressed on.

"Going to church will not make me feed my children," she answered truthfully.

"It is the Lord that feeds your children, not you," he declared.

"The Lord cannot feed my children if I don't come to the market," she maintained.

"You can't come to the market if you are not in good

health. Praise the Lord! You have so many things to answer to the Lord. You have to give him praise every day you wake up because he is the one who wakes you up and provides the sun that shines on you. You have to praise the Lord because without him, the air that you are breathing will not exist. You have to praise the Lord because he is at the moment preparing your future which you don't of course know yet. You have to praise the Lord because he is the benefactor of all, young and old, men and women, the able and the paralysed, the blind and the deaf. Praise the Lord! Hallelujah!" the pastor continued.

"Why has the Lord allowed war to begin between the Ibo and us?" Enotse queried.

"The Lord knows what he is doing," Pastor Bamidele went on to say.

"I agree that the Lord knows what he is doing. What I want to know is why he is doing it," Enotse asked, adamant.

"It is not in our power to question the Lord," the pastor warned.

"I'm not questioning the Lord. I'm questioning you," Enotse insisted.

"The blind shall see and the deaf can hear if they believe in the power of the Almighty. You must believe rather than ask questions," the pastor advised.

"What do you want from me?" Enotse asked.

"You must find the time to go to church. Now, if you can't go to church, you can still help us to maintain God's house," Pastor Bamidele requested.

"How can I help?" Enotse wondered.

"You must donate something that will help the community to continue to function."

"Which community are you talking about?" she asked.

"The community of the redeemed and the blessed," he replied.

"Redeemed from what and by who?" Enotse went on to say.

"Redeemed from the sin committed by Adam and Eve by the goodwill of the Lord Almighty," Pastor Bamidele answered.

"If the community is blessed, why does it need my donation?" she queried.

"Because man does not live by spiritual words alone but must eat three square meals a day and have the money to take care of other very important aspects of life," he replied.

"OK, I'll see what I can do to help the community," she said, giving in.

"Thank you, my sister. God will bring you more and more customers," the pastor prayed.

Orinya, Enotse's mate, decided to start attending an Adult Education Centre. She wanted to learn how to cook better, as well as learn how to write letters. Letter writing was something quite difficult for many in the village as well as in the district headquarters. Parents who wanted to correspond with their relatives living in far-away cities always asked their children to write their letters for them. They would tell their children what they wanted to say in Idoma language, and this would be translated into English by the children. The parents never asked their children to read back to them what they had written, because they trusted them and knew they were intelligent in using the English language. Orinya's ambition was to be able to write her letters herself and she decided to leave no stone unturned to achieve this objective. She would wait until her children had gone to school and then would go to the Adult Education Centre which was close to the bus station where Enotse's children sold loaves of bread and cigarettes after school. The Centre prepared many trades such as cooking, sewing, hairdressing and welding in addition to what they called adult literacy lessons. This consisted of learning the alphabets, learning the Bible which had been translated into the Idoma language, and learning how to count in English. Orinya never came home before her children. Sometimes when Enotse gave her children dinner, she offered some to her stepchildren too because she saw how hungry they were.

One evening, one of Enotse's brothers-in-law who lived in the same city came to see his brother's family. He saw Enotse offering food to her stepchildren and kept quiet for some time before asking all the children how they were doing at school. When he was leaving and before saying good-bye, he told Enotse that he suspected her housemate was having an affair with one of the instructors.

Someone came from Zaria with a letter for Enotse. She waited for her sons to come back from school so that one of them could read it to her. This was what was read.

"Mistress of my house. My study is going on well. I should normally finish very soon and obtain my teacher training diploma. We will have to move to a city that has a Teachers' Training College. I have one or two openings. I have been advised that the best College is the one in Okene, which is almost one hundred miles from Otukpo. I think we have to leave the city because we are too close to the border with Biafra. Here in Zaria, so many Ibos have left their homes and gone to their villages in Ibo land. We are told that a very powerful European country is giving them all the money and guns they need to fight everyone they consider their enemies. This is why I want us to leave Otukpo. So, you should start preparing for our journey."

Many stories about the war were traded in the market. People heard that children were being recruited as soldiers by the Biafran army and that the children were so hard and wicked that they took pleasure in removing the genital organs of all their victims, and giving these to dogs to eat. People heard that these child soldiers were trained in what some people called 'guerrilla warfare' meaning that they would hide unseen in the bush, wearing uniforms that blended perfectly with the surrounding vegetation, patiently waiting to pounce on unsuspecting federal troops. The news was that no one knew when and how these children would strike. People were told that many of these children smoked weed or Indian hemp and afterwards fought fearlessly like savage lions. People however heard that many other children did not have food to eat nor water to drink. It was said that these stayed hungry for several days and that many were becoming as thin as a stick. The news was that it was a festival when these children were able to hunt for lizards to eat. Some women in the market did not believe these stories. These, they said, were stories told only by Radio Biafra. Why did Radio Biafra not talk about Idoma villages which had been burnt down by Ibo, people wondered?

In addition to hearing about what the Biafrans were doing, people heard of the advance of federal troops into Biafra and particularly of the successes of a Yoruba army officer called Colonel Adekunle, nicknamed Black Scorpion. It was said that Colonel Adekunle's father was a very powerful juju man or native doctor. He was said to have given his son some medicine to take that enabled him to be invisible on the battlefield. People heard that Adekunle would fire away with his very special machine gun and that Biafran soldiers would not know where the gun was firing from, would take to their heels without knowing which direction to go, only to be reduced to pieces by another burst of machine gun fire. People heard that Colonel Adekunle did not like to take prisoners of war and that the Ibos knew this. So, the moment they heard that it was Adekunle's troop that was facing them, they would flee and leave their guns behind.

Pastor Bamidele insisted that Enotse attend mass on Sundays with the community of the redeemed and the blessed. His church was named the Eternal Life and Miracles Church. Enotse did not feel like going to the church but given Pastor Bamidele's constant visits to her market stall, she decided to go there one Sunday. It was a special Sunday because Pastor Bamidele had been able to convince a very important member of the parent church from Lagos to come to Otukpo and preach. His name was Apostle Godwin. Apostle Godwin was a very handsome man and it was said that he had three or four wives and lots of children.

"Praise the Lord," he began.

"Hallelujah," the congregation replied.

"Who among us here is not a sinner?" he went on. Nobody raised his or her hand.

"Who among us here is a sinner?" he continued. All hands were raised.

"This is very good. When you confess that you have sinned, you are on the right path because our Lord in his infinitesimal generosity, goodness and kindness accepts you even though you have disobeyed his commandments. Every day, I listen to and receive sinners like you who repent but who unfortunately continue to sin the moment they are out of my sight. They forget that the Lord is omniscient and that all the sins they commit are recorded. They will have to account for these on the day of judgement unless they atone for their sins before. So, you will now ask me how you can atone for your sins? First, you should ask the Lord to help you and to prevent you from committing other sins. Secondly, you must think of the Lord every minute of your life and of your existence. This will keep off the Devil and the temptations to disobey God's commandments. Thirdly, you should contribute as much as you can to the good working of the church. The more you contribute, the more blessings the Lord will rain on you. The more you contribute, the stronger the community will be and the more force we will have to neutralise the work of the Devil and his acolytes. The more you contribute, the prouder you will be as a key foundation of our movement. The more you contribute, the more efficient we will be to Christianise and to spread the words of our Lord here, there and beyond. Praise the Lord!"

"Hallelujah."

"I am told that the Congregation has received some new members. All of them have been placed on the front row. Before our altar boys come around with their baskets to receive what you will generously donate, I will ask the new members to stand up and to briefly introduce themselves," he finished. Enotse had not been placed on the front row.

"My name is Doctor Sam Idu. I am a new medical doctor at the General Hospital, and I am glad to be with you," one of them said.

"Praise the Lord," Apostle Godwin excitedly added.

"My name is Engineer Odock. I was transferred recently

here and I'm glad to be with the Congregation. Praise the Lord." A second man presented himself.

"Praise the Lord," the congregation replied.

"My name is Isiah Ajene. I own a construction company and I am glad I have seen the light. Praise the Almighty Lord," a third pot-bellied man announced.

"Amen," everyone replied.

When the altar boys came around with their baskets, some members of the congregation put in their donations very discreetly. The sums they gave were quite modest. However, others, especially those who gave higher sums of money, wanted everyone to see and know how much they were donating. This was the case with the owner of the construction company, who brought out a wad of banknotes and very slowly peeled off one note after the other under the gaze and admiration of those sitting close to him, before putting each note into the basket.

"The more you give, the more you'll receive from the infinitesimal bounty of the Lord. What you give, you'll reap tenfold and more because the Lord does not forget his sons and daughters who accept his grace and wish to contribute to the development of his kingdom. What you give, you have in reality not lost but gained," Apostle Godwin insisted. Then he suddenly went into a trance. His whole body started shaking and his feet started dancing to some music no one but himself heard. He spoke very rapidly for about fifteen minutes in a language no one in the congregation understood. Members of the congregation were told later that he had been taken over by the Holy Spirit and that he therefore had access to knowledge that was beyond the understanding of simple mortals. After his trance, he broke into a song which everyone sang, praising the

Lord and asking him to be kind and gentle with humans, to continue to guide them and to help them to continue doing good things.

Enotse was at the market one day when one of her sons ran to her shed.

"Papa is back," he announced.

"When did he arrive?" she enquired.

"Not long ago. He says he's very hungry."

"Is Mama Baby not at home?" she wondered.

"No."

"OK. Go back and tell him I'm on my way," she announced.

When she arrived at home, her husband was with a group of neighbours, all men, drinking beer and making lots of noise.

"Oga, welcome back," she greeted.

"I have not eaten since yesterday morning," he complained.

"Do not worry. The pounded yam will be ready very soon. There is egusi and bitter leaf soup which I prepared yesterday," she announced.

"You should make enough for me and my friends. Where is Orinya, Mama Baby?" he asked.

"She is at the Adult Education Centre," Enotse responded.

"Selling what?" he enquired.

"She is not selling. She is taking lessons on cooking and letter writing," she answered.

"Who does she want to write letters to?" he asked with incredulity and disbelief.

"Ask her now, when she comes back," Enotse replied.

"How is the market?" one of the men with Teacher asked.

"We thank God," she responded.

"I told the barman in front of our house to bring us one carton of Star beer. Give money to one of the children for them to go and pay him," Teacher ordered.

"OK," she said.

"I have not had any fresh fish pepper soup for a long time. Give some more money to the person going to the bar for him to buy a big bowl of pepper soup for me and our neighbours," he added.

"OK," she said.

"And send one of the children to go and tell Mama Baby that I'm at home," he demanded.

"OK," she said.

Mama Baby did not come home immediately. When she finally arrived, the neighbours had all left and all the children had eaten. She greeted her husband.

"Oga, welcome back. How was your journey?" she asked warmly.

"Is it now that you're asking?" he snapped.

"What do you mean by 'Is it now that you're asking?' When do you want me to ask?" she responded.

"Hein? So now you've started to talk long grammar with me?" he said with disbelief.

"Is it long grammar when I ask you about your journey?" she shot back.

"So, you're learning how to cook. Did your mother not teach you how to cook?" he questioned.

"I am learning how to cook for school children because I want to work after for the government," she explained.

"Who has given you such poison to eat? Who will take care of your children when you are doing government service?" he continued.

"The children will grow up and have their own lives," she affirmed.

"The children will grow up if their mother is there to help them to grow," he corrected her.

"The children will grow up if their father is there too. It is not me that went to Zaria for more than a year," she argued.

"I'm now sure someone has been feeding your head with cantankerous and highly fallacious rubbish. I'm also told you are learning how to write letters. Who do you want to write to?"

"I don't want to write to anybody," she declared.

"So why are you learning it?" he insisted.

"Must we justify why we decide to learn things? What about you? Why did you go to school and why are you still going to school at your age?" she teased him.

"There is now no doubt in my mind. Someone has been putting very dangerous ideas into your head. You will have to come back to your senses immediately or else you'll be jumping into a well of very hot water," he said angrily.

"You have not answered my question. Why did you start going to school?" she repeated.

Her husband was silent for some time. Rather than explode into a fit of anger, he went on to explain things in a low voice.

"I'm going to cut a very long story short. It was my father who sent me to school after spending six months in prison. He had a clash with an Ibo man who had a farm close to his. One day the Ibo man went to the district office to complain that someone had come to his farm to harvest all his yams and cassava. My father was taken to court and he did not understand a single word being said in the court because everything was in English. He was told to put his thumb in some ink and to sign a piece of paper also written in English. The moment he did this, his hands were tied, and he was taken to prison. He was later told he had signed a confession that he had stolen the other farmer's products. He said he would not have signed the document if someone in his family who could read and understand official documents had followed him to court. He vowed not to make the same mistake twice. He waited till he had a son, me, whom he sent to school. But why the hell am I explaining myself to you?" he wondered.

"Why is it only men that should learn how to understand official documents?" she went on to ask.

"Wonders will never end! So now you want to become a man. You want to become the man in my house," he exclaimed.

"I don't want to become a man. I only want to be able to do things I want to do, to understand things I want to understand, to listen to things I want to listen to. This does not mean I want to become a man. In the Adult Education Centre, there are many Yoruba women who are working there as instructors. Two of them have their husbands who work there too. Their husbands do not complain that they want to become men," she informed him.

"You will go to sleep in their house today, I assure you!" he said menacingly.

With this statement, he could no longer control himself. He jumped at her and started to beat her severely. He went into her room and started throwing out her dresses in the compound, yelling at her to pack her things and leave his house immediately. His senior wife told him to calm down.

She asked the children who were all standing still and petrified to go into their rooms and not come out until they were authorised to. Then she picked up the clothes that had been thrown on the ground, arranged them well and led her housemate into her room. She advised her mate to be careful the next time she spoke to their husband since she knew he had a very high temper. She told her to stop crying because the children were listening and that this was not good for their education. Then she went back to see their husband and asked him not to be angry anymore. She reminded him that once salt has dissolved in a bowl of water, it could never become salt again and that a big nose that doesn't have any nostril is of no use and that a man's strength comes from his wives and children. He listened to her without a word. The entire family left for Okene a few days afterwards.

The journey to Okene was quite tiring. The entire family was crowded in a very big lorry that transported not only passengers but hundreds of yams and so many drums of palm oil. The lorry was a Mercedes Benz L911. Its body was built in wood and there were lots of messages written on different parts of the body in very colourful big letters. One of these messages was "God's time is the best". Next to this was the sentence "Nobody knows tomorrow. Tomorrow will be a better day". Yet another message read "In God's hands we trust". The lorry was not moving very quickly because the road was not tarred. There was however a trail of red dust that followed it. There were two mechanics who sat with the passengers at the back of the lorry. They always travelled with the lorry and their job was to solve any mechanical or electrical problem the lorry ran into during its journey. The older mechanic called himself "The Chief Engineer". He said that no car or lorry engine had any secret for him. The younger mechanic called himself "Trinity". He said he always brought out his spanners and screwdrivers so quickly each time there was a mechanical problem to be solved, that he was given this nickname by his friends after a famous cowboy they had seen in a film.

At one point in time, the lorry had to go up a hill. All the passengers were afraid the lorry would not be able to make it. They heard the two mechanics advising the driver to change to gear one. The driver did this and it seemed the engine coughed once or twice, releasing some dark smoke from its silencers. Then the lorry continued to crawl up the hill very slowly. Both mechanics jumped down and one of them held a big rectangular block of wood which they called a wedge. The passengers learnt later that this would have been put behind one of the back tyres to prevent the lorry from going backwards if it had stalled on its way up the hill. The engine coughed again a few times and each time it coughed, it released a cloud of dark smoke. One of the mechanics started to sing:

My fine Mercedes
Why you dey yab like this?
Na Chief Engineer dey answer you so
Engine oil you want and I give you
Original petrol you want and I give you bellyful
Now you wan quench, abi?
My fine Mercedes why you dey do me so?
Which kind journey you wan do me now?
Which kind palava you wan throw me inside?
Which kind shakara you dey play like small pickin?

Make you no vex, o jarey
Make you show road pepper
Because na you be king of the road
And we be your poor and humble servants

The lorry made it up the hill and then picked up speed along the road. Nothing eventful happened for several hours before it was stopped at a roadblock manned by policemen. The policemen told everybody to come down from the lorry. They inspected the lorry and asked who owned all the yams and palm oil being transported. The owner, a man with very deep tribal marks on his face, and who had red teeth from eating too many kola nuts, answered that they were his. Then they saw the boxes in which Enotse's family had arranged their clothes and items and asked who owned them. Her husband said it was theirs. They asked him where his family was coming from. He told them they were coming from Otukpo. Then they asked where they were going to. He told them they were going to Okene. They wanted to know why. He replied that he was going to the Teachers' Training College there to train teachers. The attitude of the policemen changed immediately. They wished the lorry a safe journey and bid everyone goodbye.

They arrived at the outskirts of Okene the following day and were stopped at a roadblock this time mounted by the Traffic Police in two station wagon Peugeot cars. A sergeant came over and inspected the lorry. He asked who owned the yams and palm oil. The trader said they were his. He asked the trader to give him some yams for himself and his colleagues to roast while on the roadblock. The trader gave him five big yams. He then went to the driver and asked:

"Where are the particulars of the vehicle?"

"What do you want to see exactly?" the driver asked.

"Show me first your driver's licence," the sergeant continued.

"See am here," the driver went on.

"Now I want to see your insurance certificate," the policeman went on.

"See am here," the driver replied.

"Why is it that you have only a third-party insurance?"

"Oga, I never get accident. So why waste money for comprehensive insurance?"

"OK. Have you got spare tyres?" the policeman continued.

"Yes, original imported Michelin tyres," the driver answered.

"And how many wedges have you got?"

"One, oga," the driver replied.

"Aha, you are not in order. You will have to park the lorry here until you can go and bring the second wedge."

"Oga, why you dey vex like this? Wetin I do you?" the driver enquired.

The policeman invited the driver for a chat behind one of the station wagon cars. It seemed that the driver hid something inside his driving licence, which he handed over again to the policeman who suddenly broke into a very large smile and told the driver all his papers were in order.

The family stayed in Okene for less than a year. Enotse could not go to the market to buy a shed and so she sold things at home. Home was a two-bedroom house in the Junior Staff Quarters of the Okene Teachers' Training College. The house reminded her of the boys' quarters she had seen at the GRA in Nkalagu when she had taken one of her twins to the hospital a few years back. There were a dozen other similar houses close by and sometimes neighbours could be heard quarrelling. Since there were only two rooms, Enotse took one and Mama Baby took the other. Their husband spent nights alternatively in one room and the other. All the children slept together on mats on the floor in the living room. They had to go to a primary school which was a few kilometres away from the College. They had to walk to and from school every day. When they came back home, they would spend their time playing and often going to visit their friends whose parents lived in the senior staff quarters.

Unlike the junior staff quarters where the houses were close to one another, the Senior Staff Quarters consisted of very large houses, each with a big garage where the personal cars of the occupants were packed. Most of the cars were Volkswagen Beetles or Peugeot 403s and 404s. Those who owned the 404s were the most senior and thus affluent. They were not many. Those who had the 403s came next in rank, experience and importance. They were followed by owners of Volkswagen Beetles. All car owners however formed the high cast of senior government officials. The cars were washed regularly by houseboys and always looked spotless. They were usually all lined up in front of the church on Sundays and it was a spectacle to see their owners all dressed in very big and colourful agbada clothes come out of them to go into the church, followed by members of their families, equally dressed in very colourful attires.

Enotse's older children started to spend lots of time in their friends' homes with their mates. There, they were sometimes offered soft drinks in addition to cakes and biscuits, something they looked forward to excitedly. The children also informed their mother that they often drank fresh milk in their friends' homes and that at times they were allowed to watch children's programmes on television with their friends.

"I thought we came to Okene for you to join the senior civil service," Enotse asked her husband one day.

"One needs a bachelor's degree for that."

"Is that not what you went to get in Zaria?"

"What I got in Zaria is an ordinary diploma in education," he explained.

"So, you are saying we will never be able to live in the senior staff quarters," she continued.

"Who knows tomorrow?" he replied.

"When do you think you'll be able to buy a car?" she asked.

"What do we need a car for?" he questioned.

"Most government workers have a car," she answered.

"Those who have cars have them because they asked and received government car loans, which they pay back in monthly instalments. I do not want to ask for a car loan at the moment because for me, there is no need to buy a car now. When the need arises, there will be a car, by God's grace," he concluded.

The family woke up one day to find the entire college occupied by soldiers. There were an uncountable number of military armoured vehicles and hundreds of soldiers dressed in green military fatigues everywhere. Panic could be read on the face of everyone. Later on, it was learnt this was a battalion of Federal Government troops that were on their way to Biafra. They had arrived in Okene the night before and had chosen to spend the night in the college, where there was enough space for everyone. All the fields and classrooms had been occupied. Enotse sent two of her children to go and sell packets of cigarettes to the soldiers. Her stock was sold in less than two hours. Suddenly, machine gun fire could be heard very close by. Teacher rushed home and told everyone to lie down under the beds or on the floor in the living room. Then the sound of a plane flying at very low altitude could be heard. The machine guns continued to fire, and it was later learnt that the Federal troops had been firing at a Biafran plane that was being flown by a white mercenary. The plane had released many bombs that had destroyed parts of the Okene market and killed several market women. The family spent a year in Okene before moving on to another city, Maiduguri, close to the Chadian border. Teacher felt his career prospects would be better off at Maiduguri Teachers' Training College. Maiduguri was many hundreds of kilometres away from Okene. The family first travelled from Okene to Kabba on a lorry and from Kabba to Maiduguri on an overcrowded train that went at a very low speed.

They arrived in Maiduguri during the harmattan season. The weather was quite cold and chilly, and their lips often got so dry very quickly that they had to rub mentholatum on them to reduce their cracking and bleeding when they tried to laugh. The Teachers' Training College was quite far from the city centre. It was in a zone reserved for schools because it was very close to a Government Craft School, a Government Secondary School, and a Government Technical College. Mama Baby was very excited and told her husband one day that she would like to pursue her catering studies at the Craft's School. He pretended at first not to have heard her. She insisted and told him that she would go on to make admission enquiries herself, if he did not make these himself, on her behalf.

"What is all this nonsense about a woman wanting to learn how to cook," he complained.

"Wanting to learn should never be described as nonsense.

Are you not a teacher trainer?" she remarked.

"Girls and daughters usually follow the footsteps of their mothers. Did you not learn anything from your mother?" he asked.

"Everyone learns things from their mothers and fathers. But it is not my intention to live and behave like my mother in the village. The banana does not remain green always," she replied.

"What then is your intention," he demanded.

"You know it already. I want to work for the government like you. I want to be sure my salary will come whether it rains or storms. I want to be able to work during specific hours of the day and not be forced to spend all the time preparing to go to the market or waiting for others to decide how much I earn and when," she told him.

"What is wrong with going to the market?" he enquired.

"There is nothing wrong. It is just that I have decided that it is not what I want to do," she declared.

"Wonders will never end. You have decided it is not what you want to do. Maybe one day, you will decide what to do or not to do in my house, not so?" he said.

"Everyone needs to determine his or her objectives in life. You have yours, so why should I not have mine?" she said, visibly unimpressed by the arrogant tone of her husband.

"Is this what your mother told you? That you must have objectives different from those of your husband?" he asked her quizzically.

"I am not my mother," she announced peremptorily.

"I'm not saying you are your mother. I am asking you why you think you should have objectives different from mine, in my house," he repeated his earlier question.

"Because your life is not my life. You have your dreams

in life. Why should I not have mine? It is not because I am your wife that I need to have the same dreams as yours," she said, without hesitation.

"So, what are your dreams and how do they differ from mine? How do you know which dreams I have?" he enquired.

"I know you want to join the senior service. I want to join the government service myself," she replied.

"For a man to succeed in his dreams, he has to be accompanied and helped by his wife," he said.

"Yes, of course. But that does not mean the wife should not have her personal dreams and not try to succeed in them," she threw back at him.

"What will government work bring to you?" he asked in a less angry tone.

"The same thing it has brought to you. A regular salary, no sweating, no waiting under the hot sun every day, no anxiety, no unnecessary headache," she replied.

"So, you think my work has no headache," he said, looking at her with stupefaction.

"You do not have to go to the farm every morning like your father did," she commented, in a challenging tone full of assurance.

"It is not only farming and going to the market every day that bring headaches, you know," he replied.

"Maybe. But they bring lots of headaches, without doubt," she said in conclusion.

Enotse continued her trading. She sold cigarettes, bread and fried doughnuts called puff-puff, to students and all those who, like them, lived in the junior staff quarters. Her house became a beehive every morning with an incessant procession of students coming and leaving every day from Monday to Sunday. She was thus making lots of money. Her husband suggested she gave him this money for safe keeping. Sometimes he would inform her he had taken an amount or two, but he always promised he would refund each amount one day. Enotse suspected her husband was using this money to entertain members of the Agila Town Union each time this union held a meeting in their house. She also suspected that her husband was using her earnings to pay the school fees of Mama Baby, who had convinced him to accept her admission to the Government Craft School nearby. Mama Baby would go to the Craft School every weekday between 7 a.m. and 5 p.m. All the housework including feeding the children was performed by Enotse who never complained.

"Mama, how you dey?" a student who had come to buy something greeted.

"I thank God, my pickin," Enotse answered.

"How much be your puff-puff?" the student asked.

"Na two kobo for one, five kobo for three and ten kobo for seven," she replied.

"Na wa oh. You no fit give me four for five kobo?" the student asked, looking for a bargain.

"My pickin, flour cost well well and market hard today," Enotse explained.

"Ok I go give you ten kobo but you go give me gyara abi? You go give me eight instead of seven, I beg you," the student continued, insisting that he wanted to have a bargain.

"Eh? Why do dey make palava like Ibo man?" Enotse complained jokingly.

"No be palava I dey make. I just want enjoy your puff-puff. So wetin you say? Gyara or no gyara?" the student, now with a wide grin on his face, asked.

"OK, I go give you gyara but make you no tell anyone, you hear?" Enotse said, giving in.

Teacher started taking some correspondence course with an overseas institution called the Rapid Results College. The tuition fee was quite high, but he was able to pay this without any difficulty. His plan was to go abroad to the United Kingdom so as to obtain a degree. He said he needed a degree in order to join the senior civil service. Enotse did not really mind the fact that her husband was using the money she was making in order to better his qualifications and improve his career prospects. After all, the benefits that would accrue from such an improvement would go to the entire family. She however wondered sometimes why she seemed to be the only one waking up very early in the morning every day, and having to attend to her numerous obligations including being the breadwinner of the home. What use was the Craft School? Why did Mama Baby not do her own share of the housekeeping? Why was her husband buying Mama Baby new clothes on a regular basis? And why had he suddenly decided that the children of both wives should no longer eat together?

The decision had been made after Mama Baby's last son, Sunday, complained that they never had enough to eat when it was Enotse's turn to do the cooking for the entire family. Teacher had initially decided that either wife should cook for the entire family every other day, a choice that had been well accepted by Enotse but very vehemently contested by Mama Baby. The idea was to consolidate the feeling of belonging to the same family by the children who, by having common meals, would be educated to accept both wives as their mothers. All the children therefore ate together until their father decided one day that both mothers should henceforth cater for their respective children. Enotse felt this was a wrong move and she raised the question not long afterwards with her husband.

"Why have you decided that we should now only cater for our own children? For me, Mama Baby's children are mine too and I hope she considers my children as hers. How do you want to create solidarity and oneness within the family when you order separate meals and attitudes?" she wondered.

"Mama Baby is worried because she thinks you will one day poison her children," he replied.

"God forbid! And who put such an idea into her head?" she enquired.

"She says she sees the way you look at her daughters because you don't have one and she says she's afraid of what she sees in your eyes," he continued.

"And what does she see in my eyes?" she asked further.

"She says she sees jealousy and ill will," he responded, after being silent for a few seconds.

"Is that so? It is the same meal I give to her children and mine. It is the same pot I use to cook for everybody including her children and mine. I consider her children as mine. I have noticed that they have stopped calling me Mama. What did you tell her when she came to you with this story?" she asked, appalled at what she was learning.

"What did you want me to tell her? That no, you have daughters like she does? That no, you're not jealous of her? That no, she should not worry about her children?" Teacher replied.

"A man falls down with his shadow. You are taking a path that will lead to problems later on in the family," she dared to say.

"When I want your advice, I will ask for it if I think it is worthy," he thundered back.

7

"Where did things go wrong? Where were mistakes made? Have I not spent my whole life trying to be useful to others, trying to build and construct here and there, trying to ensure that others live without want, that others do not live in ignorance? Did I not make enormous sacrifices for my children, for my family, for my brothers and sisters, for the entire village? Did I not try to instil togetherness and understanding here and there? Did I not live in peace, work in peace, talk in peace and manage my family in peace? Did I not concentrate all my effort on bettering the welfare of those around me? Did I not show her mercy and understanding when things were difficult for her? Did I forget my obligations to her, her parents, her brothers and sisters? Did I not come to their aid even before they came knocking at my door? So why such ingratitude?"

"Looking backwards is not necessarily the best way of moving forward. It is not good to always live in the past, where many mistakes have been made"

"I'm not living in the past. I'm only trying to find out what I did not do right in the past that has led to my present predicament."

"What I'm trying to say is that you should not complain too much or worry about what you have done or not done in the past. You should try to see what and who you are today and be grateful for who and what you are today."

"What do you mean?"

"You should be grateful that you are not alone today in what you call your predicament. You should be grateful that you have not been abandoned by your son who is doing all in his power to heal you. You should be grateful that you have a home."

"You are a woman but you're very intelligent."

"Those who are not surrounded by their family in hours of need may complain. This is not your case. Those who have failed in bringing up their children may complain. This is not your case. Those who have not helped to change the lives of others, in a positive way, may complain. This is certainly not your case. Some are born and live their lives without any direction, without any objective apart from satisfying some selfish personal interests. This is not your case. So, you should be very grateful for living the life you live, for having the home you have, for knowing the things you know, but then you should also accept your imperfections, because nobody is perfect. What is important is not so much the energy you spend in self-criticisms but in accepting that even though we are imperfect, there are good things we can do, especially for those around us. Rather than complain, we should be grateful for all the good things that we have done or may have done, for all the good things that have happened to us, for all the good events that we have participated in, for all the good news we have heard in our lives, such as the announcement of the birth of a child. It is better to remember such good news rather than express regrets over one's past life."

8

The war with Biafra had ended. Ojukwu had fled to Ivory Coast. Twelve states had been created and the mood in the country was quite joyful. Oil money was flowing, and Uncle Ben's rice started flooding the market. There was no doubt that the country had entered a period of vast economic prosperity, but it seemed only top government officials were enjoying the benefits of the oil money that was behind this prosperity. This could be seen by the flashy and brand-new Mercedes-Benz cars many bought and drove conspicuously. Police toll gates started being mounted along major highways and it became obligatory to give what was called a "dash" to policemen who mounted such gates if one wanted to avoid unnecessary harassment while driving. The Head of State, Yakubu Gowon, was deemed by many not to possess the necessary authority to govern his cabinet and minimise graft, corruption and embezzlement among members of his team. Gowon had initially planned to hand over power to a civilian government in 1976 but after being advised by some influential and solidly entrenched lobbies, he changed his mind and announced that such a power transfer would be unreasonable. Not long afterwards, the following announcement was heard over the radio.

"Fellow Nigerians, the events of the past few years have indicated that despite our great human and material resources, the government has not been able to fulfil the legitimate expectation of our people. Nigeria has been left to drift. The situation, if not arrested would inevitably have resulted in chaos and even bloodshed. In the endeavour to build a strong united and virile nation Nigeria has shed much blood, the thought of further bloodshed for whatever reasons, must, I am sure be revolting to our people. The armed forces having examined the situation came to the conclusion that certain changes were inevitable. After the civil war, the affairs of state, hitherto a collective responsibility, became characterised by lack of consultation, indiscipline and even neglect. This trend was clearly incompatible with the philosophy and image of a corrective regime. Unknown to the public, the feeling of disillusion was also evident among members of the armed forces whose administration was neglected, but who out of sheer loyalty to the nation, and in the hope that there would be a change, continued to suffer in silence. Things got to a stage where the head of administration became virtually inaccessible even to official advisers, and when advice was tendered, it was often ignored. Responsible opinion including advice by eminent Nigerians, traditional rulers, intellectuals etc. was similarly discarded. The leadership either by design or by default had become too insensitive to the true feeling and yearning of the people. The nation was thus plunged inexorably into chaos. Fellow compatriots, the task ahead of us calls for sacrifice and self-discipline at all levels of our society. This government will not tolerate indiscipline. This government will not condone abuse of office. I appeal to you all to cooperate with the government in our endeavours to give this nation a new lease of life. This change of government has been accomplished without shedding any blood, and we intend to keep it so. Long live Nigeria and Good night."

The whole country was very excited. Everyone liked the language used by the new Head of State and agreed with him that Nigeria was drifting. People gave the example of a Federal Commissioner called Joseph Tarka who was said to have embezzled millions of dollars from the national coffers and had been allowed to go free even when someone called Godwin Dabor had sworn an affidavit in order to initiate legal proceedings against the corrupt Commissioner. This had given rise to statements like "If you Dabor me, I'll Tarka you" to indicate to people that the strong would always go unpunished even when they commit very serious offences. The new Head of State endeared himself to the national populace because of his no-nonsense-zero-tolerance-against-corruption approach to governance. Additional states were created, but this was followed by an increasing tendency to give preferential treatment to indigenes of states in terms of professional advancement in the public sector. Teacher felt that his promotion prospects in the civil service would be higher and quicker in his home state, Benue State, rather than in Maiduguri in Borno State, where he was considered a stranger. He however believed that his prospects would be higher if he could obtain a bachelor's degree. He therefore doubled his efforts to pass the Rapid Results examinations in order to go to the UK, where he hoped to specialise in Special Education. His wish was to be able to help the deaf and especially the dumb to have access to language and some intelligible form of communication. His decision to leave for the UK meant that both Enotse and Orinya would have to go back to the family home in Otukpo.

Enotse had just prepared some puff-puff and gave one each to the children including her housemate's. The eldest daughter told her they had been ordered by their mother never to eat anything she gave to them. Enotse confronted her housemate afterwards.

"My husband's wife. When I'm not around, will you allow my children to die of hunger?" she enquired.

"Your children cannot die of hunger in their father's house," was her housemate's reply.

"If in my absence any of my children gets very ill, you have the duty to take them to the hospital, No?" Enotse continued.

"Your children cannot die of any illness in their father's house," was shot back.

"Your children and mine have the same family name and live in the same house. It is only normal that they should be treated like being part of a single family, don't you think so?" Enotse went on.

"That they should be treated like being part of a single family does not mean they all have just one mother. I have my own way of bringing my own children up that does not correspond to your way of bringing yours up," the second wife argued.

"You have a strange way of talking. I started bringing children up before you were born. Are you now trying to teach me how to be a good mother?" Enotse asked.

"I'm not trying to teach anybody anything. I'm only saying that I want to educate my own children and I want to be left alone to show them what path I think they should take. There are many things I have learnt at the Craft School that have convinced me that I'm on the right path," the second wife added.

"You cannot learn motherhood from the books," Enotse

advised.

"There are so many things you learn from books. That is if you are able to understand the books," her housemate continued disdainfully.

"Books are not the only path to knowledge and wisdom. You do not ask someone to taste something that is sugary," Enotse pursued gently.

"There are different categories of knowledge. I want the knowledge that will give me more independence and I want my children to become independent as well," her housemate explained.

"We all want to become independent. We all want our children to become independent. Why do you think I wake up very early every morning to prepare puff-puff to sell? It is to have the resources needed to send the children to school so that they can obtain good jobs when they grow up. I was not sent to school at their age and I am aware that they need to succeed at school if they want to become independent when they become adults," Enotse patiently explained.

"There are many types of independence. The independence I am hoping for myself and my children is not only material and financial. I hope to be able to decide what I want to do, and I would like my children, especially my daughters, to be able to lead their lives the way they deem fit without waiting for the approval of anyone else. When I finish my craft school, I will be able to work for the government in a college kitchen, have a monthly salary like our husband, and do what I want to do with it. This is unlike you. You are giving your earnings to him for safekeeping. This is what I will never do," Orinya added, rudely.

"What I give him is what he uses to maintain the family,

to maintain your children and mine, you know," Enotse responded, gently.

"What do you define as the ideal role of the wife?" Orinya enquired, suddenly changing the topic of discussion.

"The wife is like a nut which should accept its fate of being crushed open by stone. This means she must be prepared to obey her husband and accept his authority without question. This is the way I was brought up and I'm sure it is the way you were brought up too," Enotse replied.

"Are you saying that the husband is always right and that the wife must always say yes to him?" Orinya enquired further.

"A bow is useful only if its strings are strong and solid. A woman is beautiful only if she is married and under the protection of a man in a solid home. The left arm does not willingly try to injure the right arm. A home where it is the woman who commands will not last very long," Enotse explained.

"A home where the man commands all the time and where the woman exists only under the man's shadow is not what I ever hoped for. I am told by my teachers at school that there are many countries, especially in Europe, where women are independent. I am even told that women wear pairs of trousers and that nothing happens to them. This is beginning to be the case even in Nigeria, I am told. Especially in cities like Lagos, Ibadan and Port Harcourt," Orinya objected.

"The fact that a woman wears trousers does not mean she does not respect her husband anymore," Enotse insisted.

"I was just using the case of trousers as an example. For a husband to be respected by his wife, he has to first start by respecting her, don't you think so?" Orinya asked.

"How do you want him to respect her?" Enotse wondered.

"He should listen to her, to start with," she began. "He should ask for her opinion before he takes decisions that concern her and her children. Then he should show her his love frequently. And he should always say thank you to her each time she prepares him a meal," Orinya finished saying.

"Is that what they teach you at the Craft School? To try to change our traditions and customs that have functioned well for several centuries?" Enotse queried.

"It is not what I am taught. It is my own deep feelings. I think a husband needs to listen to his wife. I also think every woman is what she wants to be or become. Life is not role playing, playing the role of a wife or a husband. Life is living freely, being free to be sad when one feels like it, to be happy when one feels like it, to speak freely and act freely. I think everyone needs to be his or her own individual master or mistress. I want to be able to decide when I spread my legs for my husband. I want to be able to decide how to educate my children. I want to be able to decide what I do with my time. We are living today in the 20th century and I don't see why I should be forced to believe that my husband is my master and that he is always right," Orinya opined.

"If you are so much against traditions, why did you accept to become a second wife?" Enotse demanded.

"I did not have many options. And I did not accept to become a second wife. I accepted to be a wife, period. And our husband told me I would provide him with daughters and that I would be free to do what I wanted since his home would become my home. I believed him."

"And has his home not become your home?" Enotse wanted to know.

"Not in reality," her housemate replied.

"Why is that so?" she went on to ask.

"I am sure you know why," was the reply.

"If I knew, I wouldn't ask, would I? Maybe I don't know how to read books and speak long grammar, but I think I understand that you ask questions when there are things you don't know and wish to know," Enotse continued.

"No, I am very sure you know why, so I won't bother trying to tell you what you know already," her housemate maintained.

"So, you think this is my home rather than yours, abi? The first wife always remains the first wife, you know. Is it because you think this is not your home but mine that you think I will poison your children?" Enotse ventured.

"Who told you I think you'll poison my children?" she was questioned.

"If you don't want them to eat meals I have prepared, there must be a reason, don't you think so?" Enotse went on.

"There is no reason. You cannot separate the fingernails from the finger. It is the mother's role to feed her children," she contested.

"Yes of course. I consider your children as mine. What about you?"

"A mother who is not yours does not know how hungry you are," was the reply.

"Mistrust is a sign of instability in a home," Enotse added.

"Well, yes, but the left leg always walks on the left and the right leg always on the right. My children remain my children and yours remain yours. There is nothing strange in my wanting to take care of mine and in my asking you to take care of yours, is there?" Orinya concluded.

"I have brought my children up to consider you as their

stepmother. They do not consider you a stranger. I don't see why your children should now consider me as a stranger. The bird chooses to build its nest only in a tree it knows well. Your children know me well and you know I'm not a danger to them," Enotse insisted.

"The child is because the mother is. Nobody knows a child as well as his or her real mother," Orinya countered.

Teacher passed his Rapid Results examination and gained admission into the University of Cardiff. He also applied for a Federal Government scholarship which he obtained. During a meeting of the Agila Town Union, he informed his village mates that arrangements for his departure to the UK were almost finalised.

"Do you not think you're too old to lead a student's life in a country you do not know at all?" one man asked.

"One is never too old to learn, to begin learning or to continue learning. Learning is a long and winding ongoing process," Teacher replied.

"Yes, but why go abroad, leaving your family behind?" someone asked.

"What I want to specialise in is not offered in Nigerian universities," Teacher responded.

"What exactly are you going to study?" the same man enquired.

"Special education," was the answer.

"What does this mean, in real and ordinary grammar," the same man continued.

"It means adapting our educational system and curriculum to cater for and to respond to the needs of those who are physically impaired because they are deaf and dumb. We need to help these acquire necessary skills and knowledge and make them feel they are part and parcel of our society. We need to provide them with access to language and communication. We need to stop heaping additional difficulties on them," Teacher replied.

"What you are saying is long grammar. We have not been able to cater for normal children and now you want to go to London to learn how to cater for those who have sinned and have been punished by God? Wonders will never end," another interjected.

"What do you mean punished by God?" someone else enquired.

"If a child is born without legs, without arms, with a mouth that can't speak, or ears that don't hear, surely this must mean that God is not happy with the child's family. If God is not happy with the child's parents, this surely means they have wronged him, don't you think so?" was the reply.

"That God is not happy with a child's parents does not mean we should not help the child to become a person, like his or her mates," someone else added.

"My going to London as you say is in no way linked to punishment or not, by God or by someone else. I think my calling as a teacher means providing knowledge and skills to those in need. Special education is just beginning in Nigeria and I'd like to be among the pioneers in this field. My chances of being promoted very rapidly are very high. What I'd like to do is to be able to train teachers who can then be in a better position to handle special needs pupils and students."

"How will you eat there? You don't know how to cook," somebody went on to ask.

"People do not cook at the university. There are many dining halls where students go for their breakfast, lunch and dinner. The meals are very well prepared and are quite cheap according to the brochure I have received," Teacher informed them.

"What about your clothes? Your children will not be there to wash them for you," another continued.

"No problem there too. There are automatic machines that wash your clothes."

"Where will you sleep?" everyone wondered.

"There are lots of hostels as well as small flats that are reserved for adult students. I will try to get one of the flats and make arrangements for one of my wives to come and see me once I have settled down well," he replied.

"Will you come home occasionally, or will you be remaining there all the time during your studies?" everyone asked.

"I don't know if I will have the resources to come home before the end of my studies," Teacher answered.

"What would happen to all the bricks you have bought and sent to the village in order to reconstruct your house there?" someone enquired.

"They will be there when I come back from the United Kingdom," Teacher replied.

"They will not be strong enough then because they will have been softened by years of rainfall," the same person advanced.

"If they are not strong when I get back, I will buy other bricks," Teacher explained.

"People in the village will laugh at you and your family. You do not send bricks to the village and wait for years before building the modern house that is befitting of a government worker. People will say an old man has left his family alone and postponed the construction of his village home in order to go and taste Oyibo butter. You have told everyone that you want to build a two-storey house. You have convinced people that you are serious, because you have sent lorry-loads of bricks to your compound in the village. People are eagerly waiting for work to begin. Telling them that they have to continue waiting will be laughed at by many. Ordinary secretaries have been able to build modern houses in the village with roofs made of corrugated iron sheets. Tongues are already wagging in the village because people are wondering what is stopping a teacher and teacher trainer, who works in government, who has two wives and who has many children from showing he has succeeded in life."

"What people think is their own business. Rome was not built in a day," Teacher replied.

Enotse now had seven children, all boys. The seer in the village had told her she would have a daughter, but this forecast was yet to become true. All the boys were doing very well at school. She was pregnant once again and vowed this would be her last pregnancy. Her first two sons were now at the university in two different cities several hundred kilometres away from Maiduguri. She was sure they would be in a position to help her financially once they graduated and started working. She thus did not have any worries about the future, about tomorrow and even about the day after tomorrow. She was however displeased by the growing distance and bad blood that was being established between her children and her stepchildren. These no longer ate together, no longer played together, no longer went to fetch firewood together. Teacher did not seem concerned by this and Orinya even seemed happy at such a development. She was preparing some puff-puff one day when the pains in her womb began. She did not worry at first. Then the pains increased. There was no one at home with her. Teacher had gone to work, and her mate had gone to the Craft School. All the children were out at school. The pain started becoming unbearable. Enotse left her frying and tried to go inside the living room in order to rest a little but was unable to get up. It seemed as if she was paralysed from her waist down to her feet. She started to sweat profusely. There was no need shouting or screaming because no one was around to come to her aid. She began to cry silently while praying. Then came a group of students who had come to buy some puff-puff. They were busy arguing about an attempted military coup d'état that had ousted the incumbent military Head of State. They did not seem to agree on the necessity for this regime change nor on the real motives of the army General that had now taken over power. One of them was saying it would be business as usual and that the outcome would be the formation of a government by the military and for the military, when another saw Enotse bent over and crying. They raised an alarm and one of the neighbours who had a Vespa motorcycle rushed Enotse to the hospital. Her baby-girl was born an hour after her admission to the hospital.

Teacher was facing some problems at work. He told his wives that his colleagues in the office were jealous because he was going to study abroad. Everyone dreamt of going abroad but only few were chosen, he added. He said he would like the family to go back to Otukpo before he travelled to the city of Kano in the north from where he was to fly to the UK. His second wife openly refused to go back to Otukpo.

"You are not planning to come with me to the UK, are you?" he asked, dumbfounded.

"Why do you think I'm planning to go with you to Oyiboland? I have my children to take care of here," she responded.

"You always have the answer to questions I ask. You want to be the man in my house, I know," he commented.

"I am not going to go back to Otukpo. With the help of some people at the Craft School, I have prepared and sent letters of application to many schools in Benue State from which we come. I have received a very positive response from the Government College in Makurdi and have decided to take up the job there. One of my brothers lives in Makurdi with his family and is prepared to offer my children and I accommodation until we can find something to rent," she announced.

"If that is what you want to do, why not? When I come back from the UK, I will ask for your transfer to the college I will be teaching in," Teacher said.

Enotse listened without saying a word.

The journey back to Otukpo through Makurdi was less trying than the one from Otukpo to Okene and from Okene to Maiduguri. There were few children travelling with the wives since many were then attending universities or enrolled in boarding secondary schools. Enotse had the time to reflect during the journey. She thought of her children and was happy because all were succeeding extremely well in their studies. The first two were at the university and she was sure that when they graduated, they would not forget her. The five others were doing very well in their respective secondary schools. This meant that all she had been doing to ensure that they had enough clothes to wear, enough to eat when they came home and enough money to pay for their transport back to their respective colleges had not been useless, she thought. Her last born, her daughter, was for her a gem. She was still at the primary school level, but she showed promise because she was always ready to give a helping hand at home. The village seer had been right finally. It was worth the long wait. The only thing that troubled her was the bad blood that existed between her children and her stepchildren. She had educated her children in such a way as to consider Orinya as a mother and to show her the respect due to mothers. Her stepchildren however had a different education from their mother. When their mother was not around, they related quite well and respectfully with her but changed their attitude once they knew their mother was watching them. The children no longer ate together nor played together.

Her next thoughts went to her husband who should now be on his way to Kano in order to fly to the UK. She had never thought of her marriage before in terms of evaluating its good and bad points. She had been brought up to consider marriage as the normal destiny of adults. It was the woman who went to the man's house and not the contrary. It was the woman who took the man's name and not the contrary. Therefore, the woman had to respect her position, which was to give her husband children and to make sure the house was kept in order. The woman's role was to support her husband, come rain come sunshine, and this meant living her life as a wife, as a dignified wife, rather than as a free woman. She thought she had lived by these tenets. She had followed her husband everywhere he wanted to go. She had not made any fuss when he brought a girl young enough to be her daughter into their household as a second wife. She had treated her as a mate and considered her children as hers. She had always avoided quarrelling with her even when she knew the other was hell-bent on provoking a clash. She had patiently engaged in different trades in order to provide the household with extra finance to complement his salary and had never had a single word of gratitude from him. It was not that she was expecting such words. She knew he allowed her mate a much wider margin of liberty than he would ever have let her, but she was in no way envious or bitter. Each time she had quarrelled with her mate, her husband systematically took sides with her mate, even before asking for details concerning the reasons behind such quarrels. Maybe her husband was excited because her mate was young. Or maybe she had given him some medicine to drink or eat. Or maybe all husbands had the same attitude to their second wives. Or maybe there were mistakes she was making.

Then, she thought of the village. What would people really think of her husband, already advanced in age, deciding to leave all his family to fend for itself and going to spend three or four years alone in the white man's country?

"What will happen if a very serious problem occurs? Who will we go to?" she had asked him.

"Nothing serious will occur. The war finished a long time ago. The children are at school with government scholarships. We are no longer in the village, so if anybody falls ill, he or she can easily go to the government hospital. No, nothing will happen, by God's grace," he had gone on to say.

"Will you announce to your children why you're going abroad?" she had enquired.

"Why should I?" he had answered back.

"Don't you think you need to tell them that you need to obtain a degree in order to have better promotion opportunities? I'm sure they will all understand," she had replied.

"No, I don't think it is necessary. I'm not asking them for approval. I think they will understand without my needing to explain things to them?" he had responded.

"It is not because you live close to the river that you know how to swim. There are some things which appear as given but which still have to be taught or explained," she had argued.

"I agree with you but I'm sure the children know that I'm not going abroad on holidays but for my work. And my work is not for my benefit but for theirs. A hen that scratches the ground in many zones will never go hungry nor will its chicks die of hunger," he had reasoned. Yes, but the hen without its chicks is not a true hen, she had thought, without saying this out loud.

9

The Otukpo market had not changed. The group of Ibo stores, selling different wares, from mattresses to electrical equipment, still lined both sides of the street that ran in front of the market. Loud music was coming out from many of them. The paths that criss-crossed inside the market, which were trodden by those who went inside it in search of the right shed where what they wanted to buy was offered, were still untarred, and some sections were wet and muddy. Enotse was able to acquire a shed and to install herself. She accepted to join a market women's saving cooperative. The cooperative involved nine other women. Each woman contributed one hundred naira every week, the whole sum being afterwards given to each member of the cooperative on an agreed rotational basis.

Though things were going on extremely well in the market, Enotse felt somehow empty and in solitude. Most of her children were no longer living with her, and her stepchildren were living with their mother in Makurdi, the State capital city. She had a daily routine: she would wake up very early in the morning, wake the children who lived with her up, prepare akamu and akara for them, get them prepared to go to the primary school close to their home, before walking to the market where she would remain until the evening. She felt alone, without any protection. She felt vulnerable. She decided she needed someone to look after her. Who better than the Lord? So, she enquired about the whereabouts of Pastor Bamidele. She was told that the Pastor was the head of a gathering of Faithfuls now referred to as the Eternal Life and Unbelievable Miracles Kingdom.

The Kingdom was located not far from the market. It was made up of several buildings that were protected from public gaze and trespassers by a very high wall. The Kingdom occupied a vast plot of land, big enough to cover three football fields. There was a very wide metal gate that was manned by a gateman dressed in a colourful yellow and green Eternal Life and Unbelievable Miracles Kingdom uniform and a white cap. This was the gate used by cars to penetrate the property. Next to this gate was a smaller gate that was always open. This was used by pedestrians, bicycles and motorcycles. There was a constant traffic of faithfuls through the smaller gate. Immediately one passed the gates, there was a large roofed shed that could accommodate at least two hundred people. Pastor Bamidele sometimes used this shed for outdoor open prayers, but the shed was reserved for celebrating marriages. The faithfuls who wished to celebrate such marriages needed to pay a fee, but no one knew how much this was. It was rumoured that the fee was quite high, since in addition to paying for renting the shed, one also had to pay for the choir, made up of young teenage girls.

Adjacent to the shed was a big imposing church with the external walls painted in bright orange colours. The roof was pyramidal. The entrance to the church was very wide and led to one central nave. Several rows of benches led to the altar that was arranged on a high stage that had been constructed at the other extremity of the church. The ceiling was decorated, and this generated a warm and joyful atmosphere inside the church.

Fifty metres away from the church was an immense two-storey house, also painted in a bright orange colour with a large adjacent garage built with red bricks in which three vehicles were parked, a metallic red 280 Mercedes Benz car, a light blue Peugeot 504 Station Wagon and a white Land Rover. This was where Pastor Bamidele lived. He now had three wives who all lived with him. The house was surrounded by a hedge made up of big bougainvillea plants and flowers. Behind the house was a large lawn next to which stood two other buildings. One was a three-bedroom guest house, equally surrounded by a hedge of hibiscus flowers, and the other a long rectangular boys' quarter that had two rooms, one bathroom and kitchen at one end, and a flush toilet at the other end. Just behind the boys' quarter, three big 1000-gallon water tanks were mounted on stands constructed with strong iron rods. These were linked to a borehole system and served to provide Pastor Bamidele's house and the other houses in the compound with water for domestic usage.

Enotse's first thought when she first visited the Kingdom was that the Lord really did wonders. She thought back at what Father Patrick had told them in the village during the mass baptism that he had done: that the kingdom of the Lord was the only way to wealth, spiritual and non-spiritual. Here was proof that the word of the Lord led to worldly riches, facilitated attaining a life without worries, and provided peace of the heart and solid protection. During her first visit, there was an open prayer session in the shed which was packed full. Everybody was singing but Enotse's attention was drawn to the centre of the shed. More than a dozen teenage girls all dressed in white Eternal Life and Unbelievable Miracles

Kingdom uniforms and blue head scarves were standing in a row, singing joyously. In front of them was another row of women, dressed in white gowns, and wearing yellow headscarves. They were all singing the song "All hail the Power of Jesus" and were dancing energetically as they sang. Pastor Bamidele, who now had a long white beard and was wearing a very long white gown with a green belt tied to his waist, was listening and swaying slowly to the tune of the song. He had put on considerable weight and had a big protruding belly. Enotse could vividly remember the Pastor's preaching that day.

"So, we now have a new civilian government with an executive President. So, in this State, we have an executive Governor who tells us every day that his one and only reason for holding public office is to cater for the silent majority who are suffering from hunger, homelessness and destitution. So, the simple question I ask is this: How many of you are happy or happier now than when it was the army that ruled? Tens and thousands and millions of bags of Uncle Ben's rice have been imported by the federal government officially to stop hunger and give original rice to us all, but how many of you know where these bags are and how many of you can afford to buy them? The bags have been given to government appointed distributors who of course have accepted to give the required ten percent commission to key officials. And the top government officials who are supposed to be public servants but prefer riding in air-conditioned official cars with tinted glasses, do they know what it is like to have to walk ten miles every day just to be able to earn the small naira that can make a whole family to be able to buy garri to drink, usually without sugar? Tell me, do they know this, do they know what the real life of Nigerians is like? Do they know what it takes to struggle to feed your children, and to buy them clothes with less than the minimum wage paid to government workers? Tell me, do they know this? And what about the police that continue to mount road blocks every ten kilometres and who do not hesitate to flog drivers who refuse to give them dash? Do they know that the role of the police is not to flog but to protect people? Tell me, do the police know this? How can you expect the police to be with the people when those higher up despise them? Fortunately, there is one authority who has abundant love and who is prepared to provide us with his protective generosity. This is the Lord Jesus, whose doors are always open for those who seek his help. This is the Lord Jesus Christ, fountain of love and understanding, the pinnacle of purity, the giver of life and the architect of unbelievable miracles. If you want good miracles to happen to you, abandon yourself wholeheartedly to his ministry. What you will gain will surpass your expectations. Today and now is the time to take the leap. Become a faithful, now! Let us end by singing 'Amazing Grace, My Chains are Gone'. Before you leave, please don't forget to give whatever you can to help our kingdom to continue to grow without hindrance."

Enotse decided to join the Kingdom. Every day after leaving the market, she would stop over at the Kingdom and listen to Bible lessons delivered by the Pastor. Each lesson on weekdays usually ended by a faithful telling the gathering how he or she had come to see the light and what joy his or her new life in Jesus now brought him or her. Each lesson ended with songs and dancing. And each lesson closed with the Pastor telling the gathering not to forget to give whatever those present could, in order to ensure the continued existence and prosperity of the Kingdom.

The Kingdom grew so well that the State Television Network decided to visit it and film one of its services to be broadcast state-wide. The Pastor's name became a household name and people continued to flock to his kingdom in search of godly answers to their worldly difficulties. Those who were poor came to the Kingdom full of hope. Those who were rich came to show their wealth, something they ostentatiously did when they made contributions at the end of church services. Enotse was so involved in church services that she felt the need to have someone to help her at home as well as in her shed in the market. She asked for one of her teenage nieces from the village to be sent to her. She would try to groom the niece in the art of house and shop keeping.

She came home one evening and found two policemen waiting for her. Her niece had been caught stealing money from one of the neighbouring sheds in the market, she was informed with gravity. Since Enotse had not been around to be questioned, the niece had been sent to the police station where she was in custody, pending investigations, according to the police. The niece would remain in custody until such investigations were concluded. This was something Enotse could not allow to happen. Her relatives in the village would be shattered if they knew that the daughter they had sent to her for safekeeping, was under police custody. What would happen if the police flogged her to death? What would happen if she came across more hardened thieves in the police station, those who sold hard drugs, those who committed armed robbery, those who lived on violence? But what could she do? She started weeping and told the policemen she would like to follow them to the police station and hear what her niece had

125

to say in her defence.

"Madame, you know it is possible to cut a very long story short," one of the policemen said.

"What do you mean?" Enotse asked.

"Do you want me to speak to you in English or in Naija?" he continued. The other policeman stared at her intently.

"I do not understand what you're trying to say. Is my niece at the police station or not?" Enotse demanded.

"Yes of course. Why do you think we are here and what do you think we are here for?" the second policeman queried.

"Which is why I'm getting prepared to follow you there to see her," she said, still in tears.

"OK, if that is how you want to behave, that's all right with us. Your niece will sleep at the police station this night for onward transfer to the prison tomorrow morning where she will be detained until the court decides to sit and hear her case. Is that what you want for her?" one of the policemen said very aggressively.

"What I don't want is for her to sleep at the police station this night, God willing," Enotse implored.

"Ok, if that is how you want to do things, that's your business. We will go to the station and will wait for you there," the policeman said in a hard tone.

Just as they were about to leave, another policeman arrived on a Honda motorcycle with Enotse's niece. He explained that the supposedly stolen amount of money had been found. Enotse felt this was a sign that the good Lord Jesus Christ, in his infinite mercy, was her protector. She thought that the only way to respond to this sign of protection was to continue as much as possible to ensure that Pastor Bamidele's Kingdom did not die.

With the amount she received from the informal market women's cooperative, Enotse decided to rent a store and to expand her business. She decided that in a store, she could sell other ware than the basic foodstuff like garri, palm oil and groundnut oil she was specialised in. She wanted to sell things like beer, cigarettes, imported wine, margarine, imported Dutch powdered milk, imported corned beef, sardines, cans of Quaker Oats and other such items because she knew that there was a growing demand for these. The only constraint was that she would have to travel to Enugu, more than two hundred kilometres away, to buy these in bulk from one of the Ibo wholesalers there. She would have to rent a lorry, go to Enugu, buy the ware and travel back to Otukpo. The Otukpo-Enugu road was one of the most dangerous roads in the country. Part of it was tarred but the road was very badly maintained, full of potholes. This did not stop drivers from plying it at high speed. Terrible accidents were a daily occurrence, but Enotse believed that with the protection of the Lord, her journey to and from Enugu would be safe.

The lorry she hired was a very big Mercedes Benz with a body made of wood coloured in red. The driver was a young Ibo man who knew Enugu very well. The journey to Enugu was quite uneventful. The boy was travelling with his mate, who was there to make necessary repairs should the lorry have any mechanical problems during the trip. The driver said he was happy with his work. He said he knew the Enugu road was dangerous but that he preferred the road and region he knew to the region he didn't. He informed Enotse that he was quite sad and alarmed at what was happening in the northern part of the country. Apparently, Ibos were being targeted once more by Hausa neighbours, who wanted to reduce their commercial dominance. In addition, some radical Islamic sects were targeting Christian churches and burning some of these down. Enotse was quite worried because one of her sons had started working in a university in the northern part of the country. Her son had not told her about the religious clashes occurring in that part of the country. Why had he not done so?

She was however happy with her children. Two of her sons were now working. Both of them were teaching, like their father. She was happy because both of them regularly sent her money for her upkeep. Like the elders say, it is the fingers that make the hand useful. She thought of her daughter who each time she came back from school and after finishing doing her homework would ask her how she could help ease the burden of housekeeping.

Her store was called Sweet Mother Store. It was located not far from the central market, on a very busy street in Otukpo. The motor park was opposite the store. This meant that the store was well located. Business was going very well. She put a big "No Credit" sign at the entrance. This was to prevent people who knew her from coming and taking things from the store without paying and promising to pay at a later date. She knew this was the mistake never to commit. What sold like hot cakes were the beer and whisky she sold. Initially, she travelled to Enugu once every three months. Now she had to go there once every month. She recruited two other nieces from the village to help her look after the store. The three nieces got on quite well. What she offered to them was to work in shifts. While they were not in the store, she offered to pay for their professional education because she felt she was now their mother and that, as a result, she had an obligation to prepare them well for their future. She asked each one of them what trade they would like to learn. One of them said she would like to become a hairdresser. Enotse wondered why and told the girl she did not think it was possible to learn how to plait people's hair in an institution, because this was something girls learnt from their mothers. Her niece replied that what she wanted to learn was not really how to plait women's hair but rather how to perm them. She wanted to learn the techniques for putting waves and curls into the straight hair of African girls and women as this was becoming the current fashion. There was a growing market in the women's hairdressing sector because many women wanted to look like the pictures of American women they had seen in films. The girl said she would open a modern salon in the city when she became older and more mature and was sure her salon would be very profitable. The other two girls wanted to become secretaries when they became older. Since each of the girls had their respective professional plans, Enotse agreed to enrol them in an evening class in an all-purpose training school called the African Queen Academy. This Academy offered training in seam-stressing, in hairdressing, in modern cuisine and in secretarial skills such as typing. The fees were high but Enotse did not mind. A promise was a promise and she was sure the good Lord would be with her and continue to provide her with the funds she needed to educate those around her.

She was bent on giving her nieces and her daughter the good education that would not only enable them to have a job when they grew up but also be respectable wives and mothers. She therefore warned them about loitering around with boys, many of whom were hanging around her home. She warned them they would bring disgrace to their family, to their village and to her personally if they became pregnant outside marriage. They were to ignore the boys. She taught them how to behave with dignity. For example, they were never to sit with their knees and legs apart. She taught them how to respect their elders. They were never to look at their elders straight in the eyes when being spoken to and were never to stand with their hands akimbo when being spoken to by elders or people older than them. They were never to interrupt elders when being spoken to and were to reserve any questions they had until after people older than them had finished speaking. They were taught to show deference and respect to people older than them. They were never to use makeup as this could be read by those around them as proof that they were easy girls. She told them she would not tolerate the slightest hint that those who lived in their neighbourhood had such images about them.

She taught them never to openly express their sentiments, anger, fear, love, envy, anxiety. They were to act, to do, to work, and to live as dignified girls and later women. This would give them husbands who would take care of them. She told them that all married women are by definition beautiful because a man had thought they were and had chosen to have them accompany him in his life. Where was the beauty in the woman who had not been chosen as a wife? She taught them how not to rush things they did in the house. If they wanted to go very far in life, they had to do things slowly and conscientiously. Life would give them very positive surprises if they adopted this slow and steady approach.

Then she made them understand the importance of giving. They were taught to always be open and willing to give without asking for anything in return. Giving, she said, procured the most satisfying sensation. When one gave spontaneously and willingly, one was investing, and one was sure that the profit was sure to come a hundredfold. Enotse did not make any difference between her nieces and her daughter because she considered all the girls under her care as her daughters.

Sweet Mother Store was making lots of profit. Though Enotse had not been to school, she decided to buy a big exercise book in which she told her daughter to draw a table with two columns on each page. One column was for what she spent on buying items and the other was what she sold. Each expenditure or sale was described and dated and the total sums for expenditures and sales were written at the bottom of each page. Enotse thus had a clear picture of how things were going. The items that sold extremely well were bottles of whisky, eggs, powdered milk and sugar.

Enotse decided to diversify her activities and to engage in the taxi business. A new crop of taxis, called Okada, made up of motorcycles, was gaining prominence. She decided to buy ten motorcycles and recruited ten boys from the village to transport passengers on a hail and ride basis. This worked quite well for some time before she observed that the proceeds the boys were giving her at the end of the day were strangely low compared to what they should have gained after a long day's work. She suspected that the boys were giving her only a proportion of their earnings. One of her fellow church goers confirmed her fears one day.

"Do you know what your Okada boys call you?" she was asked.

"No, I don't. What can they call me? Don't I pay them well and don't I regularly offer them things now and then?" she replied.

"Maybe you offer them things, but they call you 'Mama

Kudi' you know. You know Kudi is the Hausa word for money?" the woman said.

"Eh, I'm not against their calling me that. Why should I be against such a name?" Enotse asked innocently.

"You are not against that? You mean you know you are throwing away and giving them money every day?" the woman reacted, with surprise.

"What do you mean?" Enotse enquired.

"When they come back to pack their Okadas every evening in your house, do they give you a breakdown of how many passengers they have transported during the day?" she asked.

"No, I don't ask them for such details. I trust them," Enotse replied.

"How many passengers do you expect them to transport for each trip?" the woman continued.

"Of course, only one at a time. This is normal for motorcycles," Enotse replied.

"Chei! You are Mama Kudi indeed. The other day when I took an Okada, we were three passengers in addition to the boy riding. We all had to hold one another's waist so that nobody fell off the bike," the woman announced.

"Is that so? I have always ridden alone each time I was taken by one of my Okadas," Enotse responded.

"And when they tell you they've bought petrol, do you ask for the receipts?" she asked further.

"Yes, that I do. Why do you ask?" Enotse replied.

"Because sometimes, they buy petrol worth five Naira but ask for a receipt of twenty Naira. This is common practice," she informed her fellow church-goer.

"Is that so?" Enotse wondered out loud.

"You know, the taxi riders make more money than the taxi owners. Everybody knows that once you buy an Okada and give this to someone to exploit for you, you are giving the person a golden opportunity to make very easy money," the woman said.

"You mean I should not trust people who I have taken away from the street and given a source of livelihood?" Enotse queried.

"It is not a question of trust. It is a question of human behaviour. Do not forget that a fly does not spend its time eating for the benefit of another fly. Have you ever seen two monkeys share the same banana? Everybody is first his own master or her own mistress before thinking of others," she concluded.

"That is not the way I was brought up and that is not the way I've tried to bring up my children and those close to me. I tell my children that if nothing good goes outside your home, nothing good will come inside it either. In order to receive, you need to give. You need to think of the other, of those around you," Enotse opined.

"Of course, the good Lord is there to give us his guidance and protection. But we need to protect ourselves from the Devil and his acolytes. People who lie are the Devil's acolytes. People who steal from others are the earthly representatives of the Devil Lucifer. People who make easy money on the back of others are sons and daughters of evil. It is easy to identify them, pray for their redemption and confront them with their sins. This is what I would do if I were you, my sister in God," she advised.

Apparently, there were other representatives of the Devil in the city. There was a gang of young boys which was wreaking havoc at night in the city. They would break into stores, steal what they could before defecating on the floor of the store as their official signature. They were called the Latrine Squad. Nobody knew how many boys were in the gang. The rumour was that some of them were police constables who needed to make ends meet by transforming themselves at night into something that was miles away from their official law enforcement role. The rumour was that the gang was led by a young boy who was feared by his mates because he easily got into a temper and would lash out at anyone who dared challenge him.

One evening, Enotse was at her store quite late. The open market which was nearby had closed long ago and the motor park not far away was equally closed. As she was padlocking the entrance to the store to go home, she saw a group of boys walking down the street, coming in her direction. They stopped when they saw her locking the door. One of them looked very familiar from afar. Was that not Sunday, one of her stepchildren? What was he doing in Otukpo? Why had he not come to pay her a visit at home?

It was well past midnight when there was a loud knocking at the main entrance to her compound. The person knocking was also shouting and waking people up in the neighbouring compound. Several dogs were barking, noisily. Enotse and the kids woke up to see someone telling them excitedly that Sweet Mother Store was on fire. A neighbour whose house was next to the store thought he had first heard bottles being broken inside the store; he had not given that a second thought before smelling that something was burning. When he and his family realised that the store was on fire, they had sounded the alarm and had tried to draw as many bucketfuls of water from their well to try to quench the fire. The spectacle of the flames had woken many others up and there were lots of children who were looking petrified at what looked like long yellow fingers pointing towards the sky and illuminating the dark night. Enotse told her children to remain at home while she followed the boy who brought the news to her store. When she arrived at the scene, many came to sympathise with her. The flames were still big and the heat intense. Buckets of water continued to be poured into the store from a comfortable distance. Otukpo had no fire brigade and even if it had, there was no use going to ask for their help when it was past midnight.

Enotse watched as her store was being demolished by fire. The loss would be irredeemable because she had not taken out any insurance policy to cover the store. When the fire was finally put out, she was able to go closer to the store with a torchlight and tried to assess the damage. She noticed that the padlock she had used to close the store entrance had been smashed and that the door was visibly in splinters. She decided to step through the very slippery entrance and take a peep into what remained in the store. All the wooden shelves had been consumed by the flames and there were pieces of broken bottles everywhere on the wet floor. Then she smelt something foul. She directed her torchlight to where the smell was coming from. She saw large patches of wet excrement floating on several parts of the floor. There was nothing more anybody could steal from the store. She thanked those who had helped put out the fire and said she would be back later in the morning with her children to clean the store up. On her way back home, she sang the following song to herself:

When will things be as we wish?

When will goodness defeat badness?
When will misfortunes begin to disappear?
When will the road be clear and the journey smooth?
To every question, there is a simple answer
Tomorrow will always be a better day
The obstacles today tell us to work harder
For tomorrow to give us better rewards
He who wants to taste honey
Must have the courage to withstand the fury of bees
He who wants some charcoal
Must be prepared to have smoke in his eyes and nose
To every question, there is a simple answer
Tomorrow will surely be a better day
The obstacles today force us to work harder and longer
For tomorrow to make us better
The fisherman who is patient catches many fishes
Nothing comes to you if you don't sweat for it
It is not because the distance is far
That you decide not to make the journey anymore
To every question, there is a very simple answer
Tomorrow will without doubt be a better day
The obstacles and trials faced today strengthen our resolve
To make tomorrow full of promise and hope for the better
The wind helps those without a cutlass to gather branches of
wood
To make the fire needed to roast pieces of yam
No matter how small the axe is
It ends up felling even the biggest of trees in the bush
To every question, there is a clear and simple answer
Tomorrow will, come what may, be a better day
The mistakes made today and resolved

Ensure that tomorrow will be easier, happier and better
Lightning strikes the house, it doesn't strike lives
The bird's light feather floats in the air but finally ends up on
the ground
Problems raised now and then do not stop the sun from
shining
At the end of the day, what must be, becomes
To every question, there is a clear, simple and right answer
Tomorrow will come
And wash away the problems and worries of today
Hardship and misfortune do not send you a message before
their visit
But because you should never allow the plate of warm beans
To become cold before adding the butter
So should misfortunes not clip your wings
And diminish your resolve to continue flying
You need to continue digging the well today
So that you may be able from it to drink water tomorrow
or the day after
Yes, to every question, there is a clear and visible answer
Tomorrow will and must be a better day
For the difficulties faced today will disappear
And make us relish and enjoy the good tidings tomorrow
surely brings

10

Orinya was comfortably settled. Here she was in the junior staff quarters at the Government College in Makurdi. She had spent a few months in her brother's compound when she first arrived from Maiduguri and had started working as the Assistant Head Cook at the secondary school. Many of her mates felt that she had been made Assistant Head Cook because she was close to the Principal, Mr Ogori, who was referred to as Heleber because he always used this term in his speeches. When Orinya had applied for the job in Makurdi, she had not known who the principal of the school was. It was thus a good surprise when she learnt that it was Heleber at the head of the school. Though she had never met the man in the village, she had heard of him. She was surprised when she had been told the principal wanted to see her in his office just a few days after she had started working in the school refectory. Mr Ogori asked her how she was settling down and how her husband was doing. When she told him her husband was in the UK for studies, he had jokingly responded that he hoped his former colleague would not come back with a white wife. He had then told her not to hesitate to call on him anytime she had anything she'd like him to do for her and her family.

There wasn't much to do in her job, in reality. She was under the Chief Head Cook, a man a little bit older than her. He was quite fat and very pot-bellied. He was the one who made the weekly menu and contacted the relevant suppliers for the relevant ingredients needed to prepare the meals given to the students. Breakfast was usually either akamu and akara, or Quaker Oats and bread, each menu served with tea. The tea was served in four large stainless-steel pots placed in each of the corners of the large rectangular refectory so that students who wished to drink this could serve themselves with ease. Lunch and dinner meals were quite diverse and contained offers of either boiled yams, jollof rice, black-eyed beans with tomato stew, or either eba or semonvita served with egusi or okra soup. Apart from the black-eyed bean meals which had many leftovers, the students seemed to appreciate all that was offered to them at the refectory. It was Orinya's job as Assistant Head Cook to ensure that the tables were cleaned after each meal and that the plates and cutlery were washed and arranged in several large cupboards, ready for their next use. She learnt afterwards that regular orders were made for the purchase of newer sets of plates and cutlery. Apparently, this was not only to replace items broken by students but, as she learnt later, because many kitchen staff, and especially the Chief Head Cook, sometimes did their shopping in the kitchen. The Chief Head Cook rode a Honda 175 motorbike and he regularly transported things from the kitchen when going home after dinner had been served to students and the refectory cleaned for the following morning. One evening, she had gone into his office to ask him a question and had seen him arranging some cutlery, rice and yam tubers in a large sac which he later tied to his motorbike before departing for his home. Apparently, all the kitchen staff believed that it was the government which was paying for the meals and that government money belonged to them as much as to everyone else. Orinya, of course, joined the fray. She had all her meals

139

in the kitchen and took back big bowlfuls of jollof rice, stew and egusi soup, when these were being served to students, for her children at home. She started putting on weight, but this did not bother her at all. As a matter of fact, she looked forward to this, as getting fat was perceived as a sign of good financial health. She wanted to become a Mama, a woman of good standing, a woman whose physical presence told others she had made it and was proud.

She thought only fleetingly of her husband, who was somewhere in Oyiboland. How was he doing? And what if, as Mr Ogori had jokingly opined, he came home with a third wife, a white woman? Her husband would not be the first in his family to do that. Had one of his brothers, who had a wife in the village, not gone to study abroad in Russia, only to come back home with a thin skinny blue-eyed blond Russian girl? Had this brother not promised his Nigerian wife that he would come back after his studies to give her the good standard of living she had always dreamt of having? Had this same brother not come back only to engage in a traditional divorce proceeding, including asking his now ex-in-laws to refund all he had spent on his first marriage, including the dowry he had paid and all he had spent in buying the clothes worn by his bride on the day of his marriage? If one brother could do that, what stopped a second brother from doing the same thing?

She thought about how far she had come. She looked at her house. This was her house, in the staff quarters of a government secondary school. She looked around, while in the house. Her house was comfortably furnished. She had bought a medium-sized television set which stood conspicuously on a high TV stand she had bought from one of the roadside furniture vendors, from whom she had bought other items such as the sofa, the beds, the wardrobes, the dining table and the dining chairs. She had been able to equip each room with a standing fan, made in China. She had been able to cover the floors in all the rooms with brown linoleum and her parlour with a red and blue carpet. Yes, she was happy with herself.

She thought of her husband once again, and of her housemate, Enotse. The life her husband had ended up giving her was not what he had promised her in the village when he was courting her. She had vowed never to live her life like her mother, who was also a second wife. Her father had five wives, all of whom lived in five separate but close compounds but only the first wife had a say in the management of family affairs. She saw how hard her mother worked and how little gratitude and consideration her father gave her, and vowed that this would not happen to her. She had been brought up as an Obande, but there was no way she was going to accept to live like the womenfolk in the Obande compound. No, no way! Her choice to join Teacher's household had been partly informed by this: she thought that Teacher, being the village headmaster and so enlightened, would have a less traditional approach to managing his household. In addition, Teacher had told her clearly that she would have a say in how things were done in his household, and that she would not live in the same compound with his first wife. Finally, she was also secretly proud that among all the young girls available in the village, Teacher had chosen her. The pride of being the wife of the village headmaster, the only person capable of translating the words of a white Reverend Father, filled her with excitement.

Then came the war, and the flight from the village. The house in Otukpo was a single compound with two small houses within it. The houses were quite close to one another and were separated by a well. Of course, Teacher had asked her to choose which of both houses she preferred and though she had chosen the bigger, she was not that satisfied because she could not consider the compound her own. Each time people came to visit them, it was to her mate, called Ene Ole, that they first addressed their greetings, respect and consideration. She would boil and boil internally with anger. Was she not an Ene Ole herself? Did she not have children, herself? Did she not bear her husband's name herself? So, why was she invisible to those who came to her house? She decided that she would need to show she was different from her housemate. She would try to do something with her life.

Her husband's departure to Zaria gave her the opportunity to seek to acquire skills that would make her self-sufficient rather than depend exclusively on what he gave her. It was one day when she was having her hair plaited in the market that she heard about the Adult Education Centre close to where she lived. She did not consult anyone before taking her decision to take classes in the centre. Her husband was not around anyway, and she did not think it was her housemate's role to approve or disapprove her decision. It was her life, and she was going to make sure she did not spend it bending to the will of others. Her contact with others at the centre had been very positive and beneficial. She watched a Yoruba couple who worked there and saw how they related with respect to one another. She saw the man listening attentively to his wife when the latter spoke. She saw that he never erupted into anger. She saw that each time he wanted something from her, he asked her politely and waited patiently until she gave it to him.

Unfortunately, she had to end her lessons at the centre because the family had to move to Okene, where her husband had been able to obtain a job, after coming back from Zaria. She hoped that things would be better in the new town. She hoped that her husband would have a better job and that she would not be constrained to share the same house with her mate. She was very disappointed when they got to Okene and the entire family had to share a two-bedroom house. She was thus forced to live under the same roof with her mate. The country was still at war but there she was boiling over internally. Why couldn't she have a home of her own, where her children could be brought up only by her and their father, rather than equally by someone else to whom they were required to show their respect? Why had she believed her husband when he had promised she would be a queen in her home, would not be shadowed by his first wife, would not have to go to the farm to work, and would be well maintained by him? If he thought he was going to give her the life her mother had lived in the village, well he was in for a surprise. She was bent on living her life, her married life, the way she had hoped for when accepting to become his wife: a life in which she would suffer under the yoke of neither her husband nor his first wife, a life in which she would choose how to educate her children, a life in which she would not be invisible.

It was because she did not want her children to be unduly influenced by her housemate that she had been able to convince her husband to put an end to the tradition of making all his children eat together. She did not like the idea of allowing her children to eat meals not prepared by her. Did the elders not say that the mother who isn't yours does not really know how hungry you are? It wasn't that she was afraid her stepchildren would complain of the quality of the meals she prepared. She somehow knew deep in her heart that their mother was a far better cook than she was. She nevertheless felt that she was the better placed to feed her own children and was happy her husband had not refused her demand. Her stepchildren were all doing extremely well at school and she somehow felt that their extraordinary success tended to overshadow the not so bad performance of her own children. Without openly asking her children not to maintain brotherly or sisterly relations with their stepbrothers, she was able to instil in them a sentiment of wariness and caution whenever they had to deal, especially with their stepmother. She told them on many occasions that her housemate was bringing her children up in a way that would make them unable to face the hard realities of adult life. She told them to take any advice she offered to them with a pinch of salt.

The lesson she tried to hammer into the heads of her children, especially the girls, was that they should not trust anyone else but themselves to make their lives better. They were taught never to allow themselves to be trampled upon. They were taught never to undervalue themselves. They were taught to look at themselves as worthy of respect, as worthy of being listened to, as worthy of living their lives based on their principles and wishes. She did not want them to live the subdued life reserved to girls in the village. One of the reasons behind her marriage to Teacher was her hope that one day, they would leave the village and settle in a city where the bonds of tradition would be broken. She had been disappointed all along because her husband had never, for example, bought and installed any television set in the home. She believed that there were many things happening around her, around them, around the country, that she and her children were not aware of. She did not want her children to be passive receptors of what life condescended to give them. Rather, she wanted them to be active generators of their lives and living conditions. She wanted them to be able to impose themselves, to be able to hold their heads high, to be proud of who they were. Her focus was particularly on her girls: she now had three of them. They were not to accept a fate of having to say "Yes" all the time. If they felt they had to say "No", they were taught not to hesitate to say this.

Her second daughter appeared to have understood her lessons more than well. She was a rebel and was quite strong-headed. She was a tom-boy, always getting into fights with her brothers, stepbrothers and boys at school when she was young. What was surprising was that she never cried or complained. When asked what she would like to become in future, she did not hesitate to say she wanted to become a soldier or army officer. When asked if she would not prefer being a nurse or secretary or do some less risky office work, she would immediately counter that these were jobs for immature girls. She considered herself, even when she was very young, as mature, and thus ready to do jobs that needed courage. Orinya did not have much difficulty with her. Her problem was with her last son, Sunday, affectionately referred to as Sonny by his father. Sonny was hot-headed. He was tall and well-built and had a very high temper. He also stammered, especially when his temper rose and he found it difficult to get his words out. He would then lash out at those who tried to contest what he said. He was thus always in a fight, like his elder sister. But unlike his elder sister, he did not work hard at school. When he was told by his mother and father that going to school would provide the needed passport to having a better life as an adult, he would point to all the Ibo traders who had never been to school but had three-storey buildings here and there, not to speak of the fleet of Mercedes Benz cars many possessed. He made reference to all the "Alhajis" up there in the north, who according to him only had Primary School Leaving Certificates but lived in luxurious mansions, had four wives and spent their summer holidays in Europe with all the members of their families. Because he was not hardworking at school, Sonny failed his WAEC examinations and could not gain admission into any university.

Once in Makurdi, Sonny, who was then in his late teens, would take his mother's newly bought Honda 50 motorcycle and go to the city centre. He had decided long ago that going to school, to the university, was not for him and had thus given up sitting again for his WAEC examination. He would go to the central motor park where he became a tout, choosing which vehicle would be filled with passengers wishing to travel to Otukpo, post himself at the entrance of the motor park to direct such passengers to the chosen vehicle, fill this with such passengers, and then ask the owner of the vehicle to pay him the required commission. He thus made money. His mother was not aware this was his source of income because she assumed that her son was working with a car mechanic, since he was always chatting about different brands of vehicles.

On one Monday morning, Orinya learnt from Mr Ogori, the Principal of the School where she was working, that the Agila Town Union had met and had decided that all Agila residents in the city were to contribute a given sum of money for a project called the Agila Development Programme. The idea, according to Mr Ogori, was to mobilise enough resources so as to be able either to fund the construction of boreholes in the village or to provide scholarships to sons and daughters of the village who were without enough resources to continue their higher education. Orinya asked if the Town Union had women members and if any woman had attended the meeting in which this decision had been taken. Mr Ogori replied that the Union was an exclusively male affair. Orinya felt this was not normal. She therefore decided to contact other Agila women in the city to inform them that it would be worthwhile to establish an Agila Women's Union in the city. Many replied that there was no use establishing such a union since the Agila Town Union already existed. Orinya was however able to convince a few of them to start the union. She said this would be a sort of cooperative founded on solidarity between the women folk in the city. She invited all the women, even those who had initially refused to join her union, to a meeting one Sunday in her house.

The guests were very lavishly entertained with jollof rice, fried plantain, roast chicken and bottles of Coca Cola, Sprite, Fanta and Maltina. They were all impressed by the furniture in the house. They wanted to know if the sofa in the living room was "original", in other words, imported. Orinya replied that this was not the case but however informed the women that it was of very superior quality. Then one of them asked her news about her husband. When was he going to return to the country, and would he be posted to work in Makurdi or somewhere else in the country?

"I hope he doesn't do like many others who go to Oyiboland and come back with a white madame," one of them ventured to say.

"How do you expect a man not to lose his head when he sees such easy life yonder? When there is no power cut, when tap water is always running, and when you can lead your life like an 'aje butter' and there are many single women who are hunting every day for husbands? How do you expect our men who go there not to crack and wish to taste the forbidden Oyibo fruit? So, tell me, my sisters, if you are a man, when an Oyibo woman comes to see you and puts her mouth on yours, will you push her away or will you not like to enjoy yourself? So, tell me, my sisters," another added.

"Maybe our men prefer Oyibo wife because they can have children who are half-caste, very fine children with light skin," yet another woman added.

"It is not the half-caste children, no matter how fine they look, that is the problem with our men coming back with white wives. The problem is that when they come back to Nigeria, no relative can go to visit them anymore," someone said.

"That is true. The women won't even offer you water to drink, so I have been told," one of them said.

"Yes, they show you very clearly that you are not a wanted visitor. The white women think that a family is only the husband, the wife and one child. They do not understand that in Nigeria, families are large and extended," someone else opined.

"Mama Baby, you should pray Teacher does not allow Oyibo woman to give him sweets and medicine that will turn his head upside down," one of those who had spoken earlier advised.

Somehow, Orinya was not at all alarmed at the prospect that her husband would get involved with a white woman and bring her home when he came back to Nigeria. She had decided that she liked the life she was now leading, alone in her home, with her children, and not having to satisfy the pleasure and demands and preferences of her husband. Though she did not openly admit it, she did not think she was prepared to continue living in wedlock with Teacher. Nothing he had promised her had come to pass and the only time she felt happy and satisfied with her life was now, in his absence. Unfortunately, it was not the woman who asked to end a marriage, but the man. She would bring shame to her parents and their compound in the village if she went to tell them she no longer wished to remain married to Teacher. Questions would be raised about her sanity, about her maternal instincts. What would happen to the children? No sane man in the village would allow his children to be brought up by a woman who had clearly shown she was unfit to bring children up and educate them on the values of the Agila community. A woman who lived alone with her children in a city, with no sign of a husband and father around was surely an 'ashawo', an easy free-for-all woman without moral principles. She did not want to bring shame to her parents and their compound, but she decided that even when her husband came back from Oyiboland, with or without a white wife, she would not leave her job at the college nor vacate the house she had so painstakingly furnished. No, come what may, she would remain married but live separately from her husband.

The Agila Women's Union did not grow as strong as Orinya expected. It became a forum where the women occasionally met and chatted, traded news about what they had heard was happening in the village and enabled them to get to know the difficulties being faced by some, in order to see how others could help. Many of the women were always asking Orinya for one favour or the other. Many of them owed her money, but she did not mind this. She knew she would not die of hunger and that she would be able to meet the demands of her children. Her son, Sunday was becoming more and more violent with her. He was now always asking her for money to buy cigarettes. She kept a piggy bank in the form of a large empty powder milk tin in her bedroom, into which she threw the coins in her purse in order to make her purse lighter to carry. She noticed that the piggy bank was not getting filled up quickly enough as she was tossing coins into it and suspected that her son Sunday was helping himself now and then to her bank. She did not know how to resolve this problem and asked her elder brother who was living in the same city for advice. His advice was to send Sunday back to the village, where the hard life he would have to face there would pump some sense into him. Orinya was sure her son would explode if she ever told him he was going to go back to the village. The day Sunday was informed that he would have to go back to the village, since he was doing nothing profitable in the city, he surprisingly did not explode. He just informed his mother that rather than go to the village, he would go back to Otukpo. He informed his mother that he was now a big boy and knew how to take care of himself.

One of the Agila women who regularly visited Orinya was very light skinned. It was she who had spoken about half castes when the subject of Nigerian men going abroad and bringing back white wives was raised at a previous meeting. The woman also did not have plaited hair. Rather, the hair was permed. Orinya wanted to know how the lady, all of whose children were very dark-skinned, had such a light complexion. Orinya learnt that the lady was using some skin bleaching cream, which she applied daily to her body each time she took a bath. She told Orinya that the cream was very expensive, but that the money spent was not wasted since she felt a better and more desirable woman with her light skin. There was a beauty salon managed by an Ibo woman not far from the central market downtown. The woman was said to travel to London each year to import the latest and most effective skin lightening creams. Orinya decided to give this a trial.

Her colleagues in the College kitchen saw how her skin was gradually getting lighter. One of them started to refer to her as "Yellow Fever", a term borrowed from a famous song by the Nigerian Afro-beat musician, Fela Anikulapo Ransome-Kuti. Her colleagues waited to see the moustache that was bound to appear one day under her nose, just as Fela had described in his song. Orinya knew that her colleagues were gossiping when she had her back turned, but she did not bother at all. Was she the first Idoma woman to have a light skin? Was she the only woman who wanted to have a smooth light complexion? Were the others not simply jealous? Did they not also want to be light-skinned, but were not courageous enough to make the move?

"Why do you think Mama Baby is trying to look fine, like that? Her husband is not in the country," one of her colleagues said to another, after Orinya had left the kitchen to go home.

"Maybe it is because she wants Mr Ogori to notice her more," the other replied.

"Please stop talking jazz. Mr Ogori is happily married. Do you think he has the time to mess around?" the first answered.

"My sister, when has marriage stopped our men from playing sugar daddy here and there. A man will remain a man and search for the forbidden fruit in another man's garden, I tell you," countered the colleague.

"Yes, but what about her husband? What will he say when he comes back from Oyiboland only to meet a half-Oyibo woman? Look at the way she has permed her hair like Oyibo woman. Can she sleep with her hair like that? Will she not stain her pillow with all the oil on her hair?" the first colleague wondered.

"I think there is a special plastic cap that you wear to cover your hair, when you go to the bathroom and when you sleep," the other explained.

"Why all this wahala? Why all this trouble? With my plaited hair, I go to the bathroom and go to bed without any wahala," the first added.

"For Mama Baby, there is no wahala at all. Look at the way she dresses with lace to come to work. Look at the shiny earrings she wears. Look at the way she shakes her backyard when she walks in front of men. I'm telling you, she wants Mr Ogori to notice her," the other maintained.

"Yes, maybe you're not talking jazz after all," the first admitted.

Sunday was still in Makurdi. Though he had told his mother he was adult enough to know how to take care of himself, he still continued to loiter around with his friends in the city centre. Orinya had hidden her piggy bank, so Sunday had no more steady unofficial source of income. He asked his mother one day to lend him a small sum of money. His mother asked why he needed such a sum of money and he replied that he knew what he was doing. She vehemently refused to lend him the sum. He complained that she was a strange mother, willing to lend money to her own equally strange friends, but unwilling to lend to her son. He said he needed the money seriously and promised he would pay her back. She did not give in.

A week later, Sunday went out with her Honda motorcycle

only to come back and report that the bike had been stolen. She asked if he had gone to the police station to report the theft and he said he hadn't. When she wondered why he hadn't gone to report the theft, he did not respond, and started getting into a temper. Why was she making all the fuss about a mere Honda 50, he thundered? She told him to speak to her with more respect. Respect for what? he thundered back and stormed out of the house. When Orinya went to the police station to report the theft of her motor bike, the Police Sergeant on duty asked her to describe it. He asked her if it was blue and red in colour and she said yes. He asked her if she was the only person who rode it and she answered "No". Then he asked her if she gave it to a young man who was tall and heavily built and she said that was her son. The police sergeant was excited. He said the young man was being looked for and needed to be interrogated in connection to a gang that used a blue and red Honda 50 to steal huge packets of cigarettes from many shops and get away quickly on it.

He wanted to know where Orinya lived and was surprised to learn that she lived inside the staff quarters at Government College. He could not understand why someone whose parents did government work could become a street thug. He informed Orinya that he had to perform his duty. He was going to come to her house with another colleague to interrogate her son and put him under custody at the police station until investigations were completed. When Orinya returned home, she noticed that the cupboard where she had hidden her piggy bank was open. The padlock that she had used to lock it had been smashed. Her piggy bank had disappeared. And so had Sunday, who was never seen in Makurdi anymore.

11

There was a harmattan haze in Kano and at the airport, Teacher and several other passengers who had checked in for the British Airways flight to London Heathrow Airport, were worried that their flight would be cancelled. The Boeing 747 flight was leaving Lagos and was making a stopover in Kano on its way to London. All the passengers could see clearly that the harmattan haze reduced visibility, but they all hoped the plane had the necessary technological equipment to make it land in and take-off safely from Kano airport. It was getting past seven p.m. when the flight landed and two hours later, everyone had boarded it. The flight to London took about seven hours. After finishing the meal served on board, Teacher felt that it would be appropriate to sleep because he knew he would have to be physically and mentally alert the following morning in the UK. He had been told he would have to take an express train from Heathrow Airport to Paddington Station in London, from where he would have to take another train directly to Cardiff. He did not know what to expect, and so he felt he needed to sleep and rest.

He was at a loss at Heathrow airport because he did not know which terminal to take in order to get the Express train that was to take him to Paddington Station. He made enquiries at one of the numerous Information counters. Fortunately, there was a white man who was also going to Paddington station and who told him to go along with him to where they would take the train. On their way, the white man informed Teacher that he was dressed too lightly for the season. Teacher understood what the man meant when they arrived fifteen minutes later at Paddington Station and he had to go to buy a ticket to Cardiff. He was almost knocked down by the abrupt change in temperature, from a relatively warm express train coach to an extremely cold Arrival/Departure Hall at Paddington Station. Suddenly, he could not feel his hands anymore. He rubbed them together, and, shivering slightly, proceeded to buy his ticket and wait for his train to be announced on a wide board.

He sat in a coach in the train to Cardiff opposite an elderly couple. The man watched him intently for a few minutes before he asked: "You must be from Nigeria."

"Yes, I am," Teacher replied. "How did you guess my nationality?"

"With your brightly coloured attire and distinctively Nigerian cap, anyone who has been to Nigeria does not have to guess where you come from. I was in Africa for several years, in Ghana and Nigeria buying and selling cocoa," the man proudly announced.

"So, in Nigeria you must have been in Lagos and Ibadan only," Teacher enquired.

"No, I also had the occasion to travel to Kaduna in the north but yes, I lived in Lagos, in Ikoyi to be precise, in a house surrounded by a very tall wall with barbed wire. In addition, there was a man at the gate to the house who was armed and who did not allow anyone he did not know to penetrate the compound. I can't really say I felt safe in Nigeria, you know. I felt safer in Ghana than in Nigeria, which, without doubt, is a very beautiful and interesting country. I left Nigeria when the

Biafran war was beginning. So how did the war end?" he enquired.

"The war ended long ago, and the reconstruction effort has long been forgotten," Teacher explained.

"So, are the Ibos now accepted as full citizens of your country?" the man went on to ask.

"A policy of 'no victor no vanquished' has been implemented since the end of the war to the best of my knowledge," Teacher replied.

"That is good news. I'm sure you would agree with me that your country has a lot of potential. Please do not get me wrong, I do not want to make any judgement about your country and how it is being run. But I'm sure you realise that your country is rich, but that many remain poor and destitute. How come a country full of resources like yours is unable to really become the giant of Africa?" the man questioned.

"I'm sure you know that the source of the problem is both internal to Nigeria, as well as external. Look for example at what is happening in the Niger Delta region. You have lots of Western firms such as Shell, BP, Total, Elf, Exxon Mobil etc. who are happy drilling oil, making millions of pounds and dollars every day, declaring only a small percentage of the crude oil they extract and not paying attention to the wreckage they are unleashing on the environment and the sources of livelihood of many communities in the oil producing zone. I'm sure you have heard of people like Mr Ken Saro Wiwa, a famous Nigerian writer, who is fighting that these communities be compensated appropriately for the environmental disaster generated in the Niger Delta. At the moment, both the Nigerian government and the foreign oil companies have remained deaf: they are just not listening.

How come Western oil companies respect environmental rules and regulations in their countries of origin but brazenly destroy the environment in Africa?" Teacher countered.

"Your English is perfect. Your argument is well-structured and your choice of words perfect. You are talking of rules and regulations. Who makes the rules? The Nigerian government? Foreign oil companies? I say it's the Nigerian government. Now who makes sure the rules are respected? The Nigerian government? Foreign oil companies? In my opinion, it is again the Nigerian government that ensures the rules it has defined are respected. So, if such rules seem to be disrespected with impunity, the fault lies on the government and not on foreign oil companies," the man argued adamantly.

"No, I do not agree with you. I think the fault is shared. It is not because we have a corrupt government that foreign oil firms should not respect the laws they respect in their own countries. If you do not urinate inside your kitchen in your own home, how can you go urinating in the kitchen of another man's house and justify your action by saying the other man did not stop you from doing so? I do not understand the logic behind your reasoning, I must confess," Teacher continued.

"My argument is that it is the central responsibility of the Nigerian government to take care of its people. This means it is the responsibility of the government to protect communities in the Niger Delta region. If these communities feel exposed to different sorts of environmental disaster and pollution, the government, and not foreign oil companies, is the first to blame and to take to task. So, either the government is there to protect or it is not there to protect. It is when the government is absent that others replace it. These others are not public but private bodies. Their principal preoccupation is not to protect but to make money. They use different means to make this end, including those that might not be environmentally friendly enough. If the government is not there to police their activities on a regular basis, and I'm sure this is the case in your country, they are left unchecked, feel they are indispensable, and draw up their own individual and selfish laws of conduct. And do not forget that many such firms exploit the divisions and the unstable political situations in your country," he continued.

"That is true. Though we have a presidential civilian regime at the moment, we are not sure how long the military will allow the experiment to last. We are sure that the slightest crisis that occurs will give the military the pretext to come back to power," Teacher agreed.

"Oh yes, we are told Nigeria is the African factory for the fabrication of military regimes. Anyway, military regimes or not, tell me, what brings you to the UK? What import and export business are you in?" the man this time enquired with an eye wink.

"Why do you think I'm in the import and export business?" Teacher questioned.

"Dressed as you are, there is no doubt at all in my mind," he replied.

"Well, I'm not a businessman. I'm in the teaching profession, but this time, I am here as a student," Teacher replied.

"I suspected as much that you were well educated. Your accent is not very strong, and you speak quite fluently with no audible grammar errors," the man announced. "Are you here to study finance, by any chance?"

"No, not finance but special education," Teacher corrected.

"Ah, special education. So, you can't tell me what is selling well in Nigeria at the moment."

"No, not really," Teacher answered.

"I am told there is a flourishing trade in exotic wood like mahogany between Europe and Africa. You would not, by any chance, have any idea of which partners to contact in Nigeria?"

"No, unfortunately. Trade or commerce remain Greek to me," Teacher answered.

"Yes, you speak the English language very well. Well, it's been nice and refreshing speaking to you. All the best in your studies. What discipline did you say you were pursuing?" the man asked.

"Special education. Precisely, how to cater for special needs students, those who are visually impaired, those who are deaf and dumb, who need to be educationally catered for without discrimination," Teacher replied.

"Very ambitious. Certainly, worthwhile but terribly ambitious, if you ask for my opinion," the man concluded.

When Teacher arrived in Cardiff, he opted for accommodation in one of the quiet halls. Then he proceeded to open a bank account and to send the details to the Nigerian High Commission in London, so that his federal scholarship entitlements could be paid directly into it. He did not want to lose time and focused his energy on his studies.

One day, he decided to go downtown to relax a little. He decided to visit a few African stores on City Road because he had been told that many Africans had established very thriving business ventures in Cardiff and offered several wares including African foodstuff, African paintings and African clothes. The first store he visited was owned by an East African, from Tanzania. He was excited and at the same time angry at Teacher.

"So, you are from Nigeria. I met a group of young Nigerians the other day and the conclusion I reached was that people from Nigeria are too proud and speak too loudly. They gave us the impression that we other Africans must stop speaking each time they are around, because their country is the giant of Africa. We learnt that their parents are very high-ranking government officials in your country. They even offered to pay for all the drinks we were ordering. So, tell me, is it because your country produces oil that you think you are the light and heart of Africa?" the Tanzanian queried.

"You should not use the example given by a few young and apparently pampered boys from rich Nigerian families as the yardstick to qualify an entire country, you know," responded Teacher.

"No, I am not using the example of a few young boys. I have come across many Nigerians here in Cardiff and they are all noisy and bragging, when I think they should be ashamed to mention where they come from," the Tanzanian continued, unimpressed by Teacher's response.

"What do you mean we should be ashamed to say we are from Nigeria?' Teacher enquired.

"Yes, you should be ashamed. Look at all the wealth and money Nigeria has and has been able to obtain from its oil exports. Look at the billions and trillions of dollars that the Nigerian government has had as manna from heaven for more than thirty years. What has the country done with it? Tell me. How many hospitals have been built, in villages and towns across the country? How good are your roads? How self-sufficient have you made yourself in terms of food production? Are you telling me you don't have fertile land in Nigeria? So, tell me why your country imports what it eats. Do you not have land to produce groundnuts and make groundnut oil, as you used to do before? So why are you now dependent on imported vegetable oil? You pride yourself in being the giant of Africa, but you are unable to feed yourself, using the easy money you have been endowed with to ensure the livelihood of European farmers. And you say you are independent? A very big joke. Do you know that if Tanzania had half the wealth that your country has had, it would be today a very strong, self-sufficient and respected African power, which all other African countries would proudly identify with? I mean Nigeria should be ashamed of itself for wasting the resources the heavens have bestowed on it to become a world power. Rather than become an African world power, your country is the laughing stock of the Western world and a shame to our continent." the man continued.

"I am not responsible for what is happening in my country, but I am proud to say I come from there. Every country has its difficulties and insufficiencies. If you wish to judge a country you have never been to, that is your business," Teacher said calmly.

"This is what I mean when I say you Nigerians are bloody proud and think you are better than every other African. You are telling me to mind my business when I am trying to tell you how we Africans feel about the expectations we all had concerning your country and how deeply disappointed we all are seeing how our expectations have been dashed into pieces because of the typical Nigerian way of doing things," the man continued, refusing to be silenced.

"And what may that be?" Teacher asked politely.

"It is the rule of personal accumulation, of living

ostentatiously, of embezzling government funds the moment you have access to such funds, rather than always thinking of public interest. It is the rule, as a senior government official, of thinking the country is there to serve you rather than you to serve it. It is the rule of not paying attention to how the under-privileged struggle to make ends meet and break their backs trying to eat at least two square meals a day. It is buying three or four or five personal air-conditioned cars, usually with embezzled money, when most citizens are forced to trek to work, when public transport systems are kept rudimentary. It is speaking loudly and boisterously in public to draw attention to yourself. The list you see is very long," the man submitted.

"I can see that you have already made up your mind that you are right and that I am wrong and in the wrong. You should not allow yourself to flare up like that. There are many in my country who do not correspond to the definition you have just given, and thankfully so. But I agree with you that with what we have had, we should have done much more than we have," Teacher admitted.

Teacher was in his last year in Cardiff. He had worked diligently, was sure of obtaining his degree and was looking forward to going back home to Nigeria. He had been offered an appointment by the federal government. He was to train teachers at the Federal College of Special Education in Oyo. This was quite far away from Benue, his home state. He planned to first establish himself in Oyo before going to his home state to take his family along with him to Oyo. He had initially thought he would ask one of his wives to come and visit him for some time in Cardiff. He had given up on this plan because of two principal reasons. First, the cost of air transport to and from Nigeria. There was no need wasting money for a short visit to Cardiff. Secondly, his single room in the student hall where he was accommodated was not big enough to have two adults.

One of his lecturers, a certain Brian Murphy, invited him to come to his house for an evening meal. He said he was living with a third wife, since he had divorced from two wives earlier. His current wife had two teenage children from an earlier marriage, and they all lived in a five-bedroom bungalow which was close to the banks of the Taff River.

When Teacher arrived at the house, he was surprised to see that it was the woman who met him at the door. She said he was right on time and asked him to make himself comfortable in the sitting room, while she went to inform her husband that he was around. She informed him that the husband was in the kitchen, putting finishing touches to the meal he was preparing. This struck Teacher as quite unusual. The idea that he would be in the kitchen while either Enotse or Mama Baby would be whiling away their time, waiting for the meal to be prepared and served, was very ludicrous, to say the least. He saw that the dining table had been set for five. Had the lecturer invited his colleagues to come and join them? He looked forward to meeting them. When the wife shouted into the corridor and announced that diner was ready, Teacher was surprised to meet two young boys, who rushed out of their respective rooms, politely greeted him before sitting next to each other around the dining table. One of them asked what they were having for diner. Their mother told them to ask her husband, who was still in the kitchen. Teacher was surprised that the boy who was asking called the lecturer by his first name, Brian, to ask what he was going to serve them. The reply

163

he got was that they were going to eat some traditional Welsh cakes and then some Welsh Cawl to be served with rice. The boy did not appear to like what he had heard, and he proceeded to ask his mother if she wouldn't mind his finishing the meat pie that was left over from lunch. The mother told him she didn't mind at all. Teacher listened and watched, wondering about the rules of behaviour that governed the conduct of the young in the house. During dinner, he was asked lots of questions by every member of the family, but it was the boys who asked the first series of questions. They wanted to know how many children he had and listened open-mouthed when he told them he had fourteen children.

"Fourteen children? From a single mother?" asked their mother.

"Yes, fourteen children. I have two wives," replied Teacher.

"Two wives? Is it legal? Here in Wales, bigamy is not allowed, you know," continued the woman.

"Well, in Nigeria, polygamy is very current," answered Teacher.

"But why two wives? What was your reason for choosing to marry more than one wife?" the woman challenged.

"Well, my first wife gave birth to boys only. I wanted to have daughters as well, so I decided to marry a second wife, whose first two children were girls," Teacher responded.

"So, you must have two houses, one for each wife. It must be very complicated having to navigate between two homes," the woman continued.

"No, I don't have two homes. The entire family lives under the same roof, in a single house," Teacher announced.

"Is it not complicated having two women in the same

home? And the children, do they get on well together?" the woman asked.

"It is not complicated having the entire family live under the same roof. It is the fact that everyone lives in the same house that kind of glues the family together. The key word is togetherness. Of course, tensions occur now and then between the children and sometimes between their mothers, but I have always had as a rule to maintain the unity of the family," Teacher said.

The boys wanted to know how Teacher's children, and the young in Nigeria spent their leisure time. Did they practice sporting activities in clubs? Did they go to night clubs? What did they do when they were not at school or when they were on holidays?

Teacher responded to each of their questions. He saw that they were a bit surprised about what he was telling them. It appeared that the young in Nigeria spent their time working, at school or at home. Did all work and no play not make Jack a dull boy, they wondered?

After dinner, the boys left for the basement of the house to play a game of ping-pong. Their stepfather told them he would join them later. After the boys had left, Brian wondered. "It must be very difficult bringing up fourteen children. How do you know who is who? How do you really come to understand the individual personality of each of them? How do you ensure equal treatment to all?"

"It is not difficult at all because their upbringing is shared by all three adults in the house, my two wives and I," Teacher replied.

"Of course, upbringing is the shared responsibility of parents. My question is that you have fourteen children. Now each child is like a flower bud that is going to blossom. The flowers won't be the same colour nor have the same fragrance. Some have to be tended to more closely than others. The manure you give to one might have catastrophic consequences when applied to another. So how do you put yourself in fourteen shoes to avoid making mistakes that might hamper the individual growth of each of your children?" Brian went on to ask.

"Well, the cow recognises her calf even at night when there's no moonlight," Teacher replied. "It is the tradition in my village to have large families and no child has had his or her growth and personal development arrested because he or she is part of a large community."

"I still wonder how a very well-educated man like you should remain traditional. You do not have a family because you want to respect an old tradition but because you want to be able to have offspring and give them the necessary resources and attention for them to become autonomous adults. I continue to believe that it is not the quantity of children we have that is important but the quality of the education and values we give them," Brian argued. "Do you have family planning services in Nigeria?" he inquired.

"None that I'm aware of. A child in Nigeria is a gift from heaven. Having lots of children in my village means that you have several eyes. It means you are sure that you will be well taken care of when you become old. No, I'm not aware of any family planning service, but even if there were one, not many Nigerians would go to it for advice. You don't ask a stranger to indicate to you how many children you should have. A child who is born has a mother. The child who has a mother never dribbles," Teacher explained.

"So, it means the mother has more child-rearing work than the father," Brian concluded.

"No, both parents have equally important roles. The bird does not fly with only one wing and all elephants have two tusks," Teacher argued.

Brian did not appear to be convinced by Teacher's explanations. He was lost in deep thought when Teacher spoke once more.

"How come you allow your stepson to call you by your first name?"

Brian was taken aback for a few minutes before he answered.

"What is wrong with that?"

"Well, you don't call your father, your mother, your stepfather, your stepmother or anyone in your family that is part of an older generation by their first names," Teacher explained.

"And why can't you?" Brian enquired with incredulity.

"Because calling people by their first names expresses proximity and familiarity. Familiarity with the young breeds contempt rather than respect," Teacher explained.

"It is not because you call someone by his or her first name that you do not respect the person. So how do you want my stepsons to call me?" Brian wondered.

"Father or Papa," Teacher replied.

"But I am not their father," Brian queried.

"Biologically speaking, you are right. But the role you're performing is the role of a father. So, your stepsons should address you on that basis," Teacher continued.

"My stepsons respect me. I should also add that I respect them. I respect their opinions. I respect their privacy. I respect their feelings. What counts is the mutual respect we have for one another. The mutual respect my wife and I have for one another. This is what counts, rather than how I am addressed," Brian said.

"I respect what you say, but I strongly believe that there should be some form of distance between parents and their children. When I was a child, I never ate with my father, nor with my mother, come to think of it. I have personally never eaten with my children. Neither have I eaten with my wives. I have always eaten alone, except when other men are guests in the house, and we eat together. I think distance generates respect," Teacher contended.

"Respect comes from knowledge. Respect comes from knowing who the other really is in order to better appreciate him or her. If you maintain distance, you do not know the other. What you think is respect is to my mind rather fear. Don't you think your wives fear you? Don't you think your children fear you? Do you really know your children? Do you really know your wives? Do you think they know you, know your dreams, know your fears, know your opinion on events happening in your country and around the world? My wife and stepsons know me, because we spend time together. I play scrabble occasionally with my wife and we go to the cinema together regularly. I play ping-pong at least twice a week with my stepsons and we usually engage in very lively discussions on a wide range of issues, from fashion and music to youth unemployment, racism and growing fast food restaurants. I learn many things from them because they speak openly with me. I do not in any way wish to create any distance between them and I. Though they are not my children biologically as you have said, I consider them my children all the same and would be extremely sad the day they would consider me a distant stranger," Brian asserted.

"What you're saying makes sense only in Western Europe, in my opinion. When my brothers come to visit me in my house, my children do not call them by their first names. They address their uncles respectfully by saying "Sir," Teacher spelt out.

"Why such a formality? Why 'Sir', when what is required is natural chit-chat between people?" Brian questioned.

"Formality is not the word I would use. Customary and normal would be more appropriate," Teacher responded.

"If you believe addressing someone very formally is a way of engaging in a natural conversation, then I think different codes of communication exist in both our countries," Brian conceded. "Every country, community and culture have its own particular norm and codes of conduct. I think we should all be open-minded enough to accept that others might not think and do and act like we do. Which is what makes the world a particularly interesting place to learn about and if possible, visit. Knowing how others behave very differently from how we do makes us better humans because it makes us more tolerant. It has been very instructive discussing with you this evening," Brian concluded.

Teacher was deep in thought when he walked back to his room. He reflected on what Brian had said concerning knowing members of his family. Of course, he knew them, didn't he? He wondered for a while. What did Brian mean when he raised the question of knowing? Was he suggesting that if one did not chat with one's children, one did not know them and that one was consequently a bad parent? He reflected on his own father. Had his father, the gods bless his memory, not shown good fatherliness by being reliable, protective, and doing all he could to ensure that his many children were well fed? Even if he admitted that his own mother almost broke her back in her effort to make sure her children did not suffer from want, was this effort not successful only because his father had given her a home and a name? What would his children think if, when he went back to Nigeria, he authorized them to eat with him? Word would go round that he had lost his head and senses in Oyiboland. What would people think if he started having meals with his wives? I mean, what would he chat about with his wives during the meal, he asked himself? How to plait one's hair? The gossip about so and so's wife? Tuffia! No way! he resolved.

Teacher however admitted that it had been worth the while coming to Cardiff. He had learnt to be patient, less grumpy and more able to contain his temper. He had learnt to live with some of his neighbours, one of whom would play his electric guitar for hours on end. He had proven to himself that he was capable of learning new things, of adapting himself to a totally different educational culture from what he had seen in Zaria. Here in Cardiff, he had to work more autonomously than in Zaria, had to do more unmonitored personal research and work. The time flew quickly, and he hardly had the luxury of being home-sick, except of course sometimes when he was not happy with the meals served at the restaurant close to his hall. He was looking forward to going back to Nigeria and taking up his post in Oyo. This was a region he did not know and had never been to. It was in Yorubaland. The Principal of the College he was going to work in was a Yoruba man. The Vice-Principal was also a Yoruba man. As a matter of fact, most of the key officers in the College, such as the Bursar, were all Yoruba men. This was the direct result of the policy of indigeneity that was being applied by the Nigerian government, which meant that the key senior officers in federal institutions in a state were more than likely to be indigenes of the state. Teacher did not really know what to think of this policy. As long as able and experienced hands were chosen to run things, there was no problem with recruiting such hands from an area referred to as the "Catchment Area" of the institution in question. But then, were all the hands recruited as able as they should be? Was experience not sometimes sacrificed on the altar of satisfying the "Catchment Area"? Anyway, as long as the College could offer him the most conducive environment to do his teaching, he would be happy with whoever was in charge of running its affairs.

He hoped the College had a senior staff quarter where he would normally be. He hoped his house would have a big boys' quarter, where his children could sleep when they came visiting or on holidays. He then thought of his wives. He was sure they were doing fine. He had heard no bad news from home. The only news he had heard concerned things happening at the national level. It appeared the Second Republic had fallen because the military were dissatisfied with the blatant corruption that had become the norm in the way governments were being run. They had decided to take over power and wage a national war against indiscipline. Teacher thought about the Tanzanian he had met and wondered if the Tanzanian had not been right after all. How could the promise of a great country be dashed to pieces due to the greed of a few powerful ones?

He thought particularly of his second wife. What a strong-headed woman he had married. A woman full of surprises, with an independent streak that he found sometimes annoying but also amusing. What a tough-willed woman! When he was courting her, she had never appeared meek, but he had never suspected she was so independent in spirit, never afraid to contest his authority or his will. She would surely now be working in the college refectory in Makurdi. He would try to see how she could be transferred to the College of Special Education in Oyo. He looked forward to reuniting his family once again.

12

Teacher had been in Oyo for now almost ten years. He would soon retire from the federal civil service and so leave Oyo for Otukpo. Things had not really gone according to what he had planned when he came back from Cardiff. He had spent an entire year in a three-bedroom house close to the noisy Oyo motor-park before he was finally allocated a bigger house in the senior staff quarters. Unfortunately, the house had no boys' quarter. He went to see the College Principal to find out if his second wife could be employed in the college kitchen. The principal told him that the college was facing serious financial difficulties because of austerity measures applied by the federal government and that consequently, all new appointments had been frozen, sine die. Teacher drew the principal's attention to the Vice-Principal's wife who had been recruited a week earlier as Assistant Librarian, but the principal asked him to stop being arrogant and telling people how things should be run in the college. This was Oyo and not Cardiff, he was informed. Teacher had gotten on the nerves of many. This was even more so as he told anyone who cared to listen to him that he was a prince. He would proudly indicate that his father had been the most powerful member of the Council of Chiefs in his village. He would sign "Prince" in all his correspondence. When asked why he was hell-bent on drawing attention to his background, he would give the examples of many others in the country who placed titles such as "Chief", "Alhaji", "Dr" or "Senator" in front of their names. He argued that it was only normal and natural for him to announce who he was and what station he was born into. Many of his colleagues made fun of him, when he was not with them. They wondered for example what he had done with all the money he must have saved when he was in Cardiff. Did all the people who went abroad to study not come back with brand new air-conditioned Mercedes Benz cars? Why had the prince not come back home with one? Rather, he had bought a light-blue second-hand Peugeot 504 station wagon that always had a long trail of dense blue smoke following it when it was being driven. There was even a song about Prince and his jalopy that was sung each time Teacher left the staffroom on his way home:

Everybody stand up, bow and kneel down
To salute kabiyesi and his jalopy speeding by now
Blue smoke closely trailing as royal signature
Informing those of us ignorant of the princely nature
Of the intelligence of he who speaks Queen's English
A world apart from our pidgin rubbish
There goes Mister knows-all, Master of all
Prince and his jalopy, both rolling as a ball
Tyres worn out
Silencer like a loud mouth
Brake out of order
Panel beat body an original wonder
Ah let's all stand still like soldiers to attention
And give kabiyesi the respect that goes with his function
And pray that Mr Prince and his jalopy
Will come and do us gra-gra again tomorrow with alacrity.

Teacher's colleagues were also surprised that he was living alone. Where were his two wives? Where were all the children he boasted of regularly? If he was a prince and had many children who were now working at senior service positions as he proudly claimed, how come he did not have a houseboy or housegirl with him, someone to do the cooking, the washing and the ironing? Because there were times it was clearly visible that the agbada he was wearing was crumpled and hardly spick and span.

Teacher however never allowed himself to have his feathers ruffled by the problems he encountered initially in Oyo. He patiently waited to be allocated a better and bigger house. He had gone to his home state after he had been given the three-bedroom house close to the motor-park and had asked both wives to come and join him in his new location. His second wife had told him blankly that she was not going to leave her job in Makurdi to go and waste her time in Oyo. She had said she was hoping to be made Head Cook sooner or later and felt that resigning from her job was the last thing she was going to do. Teacher saw that she now had permed hair, had become lighter in complexion and had put on some weight. He had tried to convince her that he needed his family with him in Oyo, but she had remained adamant in her refusal. He had made the same demand to his first wife, who had also been very reserved about moving to Oyo. This was in the heart of Yorubaland, was it not? Was the region safe? Was it not close to Lagos, where there was enormous violence and insecurity? Would she be able to trade there? And since he was residing only temporarily in the house he had been given, would it not be better to wait until he had a bigger and better house before bringing his family to join him there in Oyo?

Living alone in Oyo was difficult. There was no one to do the cooking, to clean the house, to wash the clothes and iron them. None of his children lived with him. The older ones either had jobs in other cities in the country, or were enrolled in various colleges or universities here and there, but far from Oyo. When those still at school had their holidays, they preferred to spend them with their older brothers or sisters already working in the big cities. So, Teacher had to take care of himself, as best as he could. This was something new to him. He had never had to take care of himself. His meals had always been prepared and served to him. When he was in Cardiff, he only needed to walk for a few minutes to the restaurant close to his hall of residence to choose from a wide range of menus. There was a launderette with many washing and drying machines close to the same hall, where he took his clothes for washing at a very low price. So even when he was in Cardiff, he had not cooked.

Now in Oyo, Teacher had to find a way to feed himself and maintain his house. For his meals, he initially chose to take his lunch and dinner in a bukateria close to the motor-park but after a while, he decided to eat there only once a day. Then, after a while, he decided that he would have to do some light cooking at home. He bought a kerosene cooker, some kitchen utensils and cooked simple boiled rice or boiled yam dishes which he ate with tomato ketchup. Thrice a week, he would go to the Oyo Club, of which he was a member, and would order a plate of pepper soup and a bottle of beer. His favourite brand was Star Beer.

Teacher was finally allocated a bigger and better house in the senior staff quarters, close to the Oyo Club. He travelled to his home state full of hope of coming back with his wives and children this time around. His second wife received him well in Makurdi but again told him calmly that going to live in Oyo was out of the question for her. He reminded her that it was customary for the wife to follow her husband wherever he went, and she replied that that was pre-colonial and colonial mentality. Had he not gone to the UK? She was not going to leave Makurdi. If he wanted to come and visit her now and then, he was welcome to do this, but she was remaining put where she was working. His discussion with his first wife, Enotse, was more positive. She agreed to abandon her commercial activities in Otukpo and follow her husband to Oyo. She felt it was her duty. Did the elders not say that the strength of a bow came from its string? So, was the man not the string in the family? Though she was apprehensive about how she was going to live in Yorubaland, she accepted to join her husband in Oyo.

She was appalled at the state of the house when she first arrived. It took her some time to make it more accommodating and more hygienic. Then boredom set in, she was not used to being alone in a house, and when her husband left on weekdays to go to work, she spent the whole day idle, doing nothing. Her husband had not even bought a television set, so she could not watch any programmes on television. When she asked him why he hadn't bought a television set, he said it was too expensive. She drew his attention to the fact that they could not offer even a glass of cold water to anyone who came to visit them in their house because they had no refrigerator. Why hadn't he bought one, she asked him one day. He replied that it was too expensive and that he did not see the need in buying one. She asked another day what he was doing with all the money he was earning, now that he was part of the senior service. He told her he was saving in order to contest the village chieftaincy title after his retirement.

"You will need lots and lots of money for that. You will have other very rich men in the village who have built very big colourful storey houses in the village. Do you think people will take you seriously, since you have not even been able to finish building your house in the village?" she told him.

"You know all the building blocks I ordered home before I left for the UK were stolen. Now that one of my younger brothers has constructed a house in our compound, I consider his house our family house," Teacher responded.

"It is, no matter how you look at it, not your own house. I will not feel at ease in it," she continued.

"It is the family house. I brought my younger brother up, paid his school fees when he was younger. He spent all his holidays in our home. So why should I not feel at ease staying in the house he has built in the village?" Teacher countered.

"It is just that someone you brought up has been able to build a house while you have not. People are talking in the village," she maintained.

"People will always talk in the village, whatever you do. Even here in Oyo, people are talking. Well, I have my own plan. When I retire from the civil service, I want to become the District Head of our village and district," Teacher responded. "I will feel idle and bored if I don't have something to do, meetings to hold, decisions to take and so on and so forth."

"There is too much bad blood in the village. Even if you are able to obtain the title, those that will have spent more than you to obtain it and are not chosen by the Council of Chiefs will bear you ill will and try to poison you," she went on to say.

"My colleagues here bear me ill will already, maybe because I'm not a Yoruba man or maybe because I went to the UK for my studies. That has not stopped me from doing my job," Teacher responded.

"It is difficult to compare strangers and people you don't know bearing you ill will, and people you know and have related to all your life having the same feelings towards you. Life in the village is not easy and being the village head even less so," she argued.

"That I will have enemies in the village is as clear as the sun that rises every day. The moon illuminates the night, but it leaves some corners in darkness. It will be impossible to satisfy everyone. What is important is what I plan to do for the village and how I plan to lead. The tail of the cow goes to the left and then to the right and then to the left and then to the right again continuously. The moment I take care of all, what my enemies say and do will have no effect on me. Even if the elephant is thin, he remains the king of the forest," Teacher explained.

"The question is the huge amount of money you will have to spend. I have the impression you don't know to what extent you have to spend money. You will have to regularly visit members of the Council of Chiefs and during each visit, you can't go empty-handed. You will have to give each one presents that are worth their rank. Crates of soft drink, cartons of beer, bottles of imported red wine, bottles of original whisky, not the whisky made from mixing kai kai and Fanta and so on and so forth. And I'm not talking of the banknotes you have to give each one visited at the end of the courtesy visit. And you are not sure you will be chosen. You are making sacrifices today in order to obtain something very expensive tomorrow, and which, I repeat, you are not sure of obtaining, anyway," she contended.

"Something very expensive, you say. My children are there to help me have the needed money to pursue my objective," Teacher reasoned.

"Your children? Why involve your children in this? Have you already spoken to them about it?" she asked.

"No, I haven't, and I don't need to. When the time comes, I will inform all of them. I will draw up a formula that will indicate how much each is to contribute, depending on how long they have been working," Teacher replied.

"I don't know if they will take kindly to not being informed now and of only being asked to send you money at the last minute to satisfy your kingship ambitions. They are no longer children you know. Some of them have their families and children and have more pressing concerns than your desire to become District Head," she affirmed.

"My objective is in reality theirs. The glory I will have will shine on them. So, they will be contributing to their own greatness too," he declared.

"They are no longer children, I repeat. I know my children very well. I do not know Mama Baby's as much. I'm sure you've heard about Sonny. Do you think the village will accept to have the father of a notorious and imprisoned criminal as its head?" Enotse queried.

"Sonny is in prison, but he is now a man. He cannot be educated anymore. The fisherman who throws his net into the river when all the fish have already gone will be wasting his time. Sonny is like his mother, very hot-headed. But, all parents have children who do not follow their footsteps.

Normally, the calf follows the cow, just like the hindlegs of a dog follow its forelegs. Sometimes, this law is not obeyed. Sonny was not well brought up by his mother and this is the result. But that won't stop me from pursuing my dream," Teacher confided.

"So, when will Sonny's mother be here?" she asked.

"She is very strong-headed. She has decided to stay in Makurdi," Teacher answered.

"So, what are you planning to do?" Enotse enquired.

"Nothing. I will travel to Makurdi once in a while to see her," he answered.

"You complain you don't have money, yet you're willing to spend money to travel more than a thousand kilometres to see a wife that doesn't want to follow her husband. People are talking in the village you know," she said.

"People will always talk in the village no matter what you do," Teacher replied.

The more his date of retirement approached, the more obsessed Teacher became by his dream to become the next District Head of his village. The current District Head was from a family that had provided more than ten District Heads since the village was founded. This family would fight very hard to keep the headship within it. It was Mr Ogori, Heleber's family. There was talk that Heleber's elder brother was being groomed to take over the mantle of village leadership should their father die. Though the Council of Chiefs had to make the final choice, everyone thought that it was a foregone conclusion that the Ogoris would continue to head the village and its district. This did not deter Teacher from having high hopes. His father had been a very powerful member of the Council of Chiefs and so he believed he had every right, as the

Ogoris, to seek the village leadership.

Enotse was idle. She would wake up, prepare her husband's meals and clean the house. She asked her husband to employ a houseboy to clean the house, but he refused, saying that the houseboy would have to be paid and that he was not prepared to throw money out of the window in such a manner. The boys' quarter behind the house thus remained empty for most of the time, since the children rarely went to Oyo during their holidays. So, there was nobody to speak to in the house once her husband left home in the morning. Enotse was thus idle. She was not used to not doing something, not speaking to people, not having people around her. She thought about joining a church, but she did not want to join the Aladura, dominant in Yorubaland. She had heard that the Aladura engaged in what they called spiritual healing and were often dressed in white. This, she did not like. So, she stayed at home, idle, and spent her time eating. She once tasted a glass of Beefeater gin from a bottle her husband had left on the table in the living room. She did not like the taste and spat what was in her mouth outside the house. She was idle, stayed at home, ate, took care of her husband and waited for him to retire so that she could finally move back to Otukpo.

Teacher was idle. He had been retired for more than a year and he was now in his compound in Otukpo. His compound looked abandoned. The corrugated iron sheets that were on the roof of his two houses had turned rusty brown and the white painting on the walls almost worn out. Five of his children had now built modern mansions in the Government Residential Area (GRA) in Otukpo, all with boys' quarters and one of them had offered him accommodation in his house, but he had chosen not to leave his own compound. All five children with houses were from his first wife. His second wife, who had finally agreed to come and join him in Otukpo, had said she would not like to live in a house that belonged to her stepchildren. So, Teacher lived in his own compound. He would wake up in the morning, ask that his armchair be brought out if it was not raining, and would sit in the veranda, looking at passers-by walking along the street that ran in front of his house. Some passers-by would see him, come over and greet him and they would chat for some minutes before they finally left. Sometimes, elders came from the village to visit him. He would offer them food and drinks and chat with them until they left in the evening. Though he enjoyed such expression of respect, this was not the post-retirement life he had planned for. The incumbent village head, an Ogori, though gravely ill, was still at the helm of village affairs.

So, Teacher was idle, his daily life organised around the routine of waking up in the morning and sleeping at night, while doing nothing planned and specific in-between. One day, three titled elders from the village came to see him. They chatted for a while about things that were happening at the national level. They talked about the heavy-handed military government that had sentenced several key leading Ogoni figures in the Niger Delta region to death for treason and wondered what was going to become of the country. They talked about the Boko Haram Islamic sect that was unleashing mayhem in the north-eastern part of the country and wondered what was going to become of the country. Then they talked about the state of the road between the village and Otukpo. They had had to spend more than four hours in a Toyota HiAce commercial vehicle to ply the seventy-kilometre untarred road that separated their village from Otukpo. What had the state government done with all the funds it was receiving from the federal government, they wondered. How come their village had remained neglected for so long, they wailed. What was going to become of the village if it continued to be ignored, they complained. Then one of them coughed slightly and said in a low voice,

"Have you heard the noise that has happened?"

"What noise?" Teacher asked.

"The noise in the village. Ogaba Idu Ogori has gone to join our ancestors. He is now a spirit and is at present among the many that travel with the winds to make us breathe," the man responded.

"Why did no one know about this before now?" Teacher wondered.

"As a matter of fact, Ogaba Idu Ogori left more than six months ago. It is the tradition in the village not to announce the departure of an Ogaba Idu for as long as possible, so that the fight for his succession does not pollute the period of grief that the Council of Chiefs is entitled to have. It is being planned in the village to celebrate his life and his departure. The masquerades will come out and dance and all the age grades, both men and women, will come out in their traditional attires and sing and dance for at least a week. People will eat, and drink, and dance. Your name has been floated as a possible successor to the throne. You should know that yours is not the only name being whispered here and there. Anyway, you will have to show your strength and willingness by participating in the purchase of all that is needed for Ogaba Idu Ogori's celebration. We will need to buy seven cows, ten goats, and lots of tolotolo. We have come here to ask you if you are ready," the man concluded.

"You have come well," Teacher responded. "As you will always find your mouth when you eat in a very dark room, so is it normal for me to help make Ogaba Idu Ogori's departure a huge success. Yes, you can count on me."

"We knew we could count on you. You will now be able to show us your strength and will," the man affirmed.

Teacher sent one of the teenage children in the house to go and buy a goat which was killed. A lavish meal was prepared for the elders. They would report back to members of the Council of Chiefs that they had been royally catered for by him. He was a strong man and he was hell-bent on proving this to those that mattered.

Ogaba Idu Ogori's celebration was a monumental success. There was abundant food for all to eat. The village elders rejoiced at being able to quench their thirst with the bottles of original whisky that were passed along from one person to the other as they sat in the big shed that had been built in the compound of the late village head. They chatted noisily about how his reign had been peaceful. Skirmishes had occurred now and then between the village and surrounding Eza communities, but no violence had erupted between the neighbours. Then some of them wanted to know which among them could last the longest after drinking whisky without passing out. Jollof rice was eaten, goat meat pepper soup "dealt with", as they used to say, and glasses of whisky gulped down. They thanked the sons of the village that had made it possible to organise such a befitting ceremony for the departure of the village head.

The Council of Chiefs was undecided on who to choose as the new village head. There were two serious contestants, Teacher, and Heleber's elder brother. The Ogoris had lots of arguments in their favour. These included their experience in royal matters, their enormous wealth and the fact that they had the blessing of a very important son of the village, a certain Chief Okibe, who was a thriving businessman in Abuja, the capital city of the country. Chief Okibe was the de facto head of the Council of Chiefs. He had been a top federal government official in the Ministry of Petroleum for almost two decades before he retired, had been able to construct many luxurious houses in Abuja which he let to European companies wishing to offer accommodation to their staff deployed to Nigeria and was known to be on first-name terms with many past Nigerian Presidents. His approval was thus capital for anyone wishing to ascend to the office of Village and District Head. The pro-Teacher's members of the council underlined the fact that he was well-lettered, that he had been to various parts of the country, including going abroad and thus that he would know how to speak to officials at the state and federal levels to make them do things in the village. Those against Teacher's candidacy drew their attention to the fact that he was unable to instil discipline in his own family. Did his second wife not live far away from him for a long period? Was one of his sons not in prison? Those in favour of Teacher countered that what mattered about wives was how the first wife, the Ene-Ole, behaved, and not how all other wives did. Had Enotse not proven for ages that she was a real woman, capable of taking care of Teacher's house, which would become everyone's house, if Teacher became village head? As for his child in prison, did our elders not say that a centipede with one broken leg continues to walk and get to his house? they affirmed.

One of the members of the Council of Chiefs, who had

argued in favour of Teacher's candidacy, told him he had to contact Chief Okibe in Abuja and ask the Chief to accept to become his godfather. Contact was made and an appointment arranged in the Chief's house in Abuja.

"Welcome to my home, Teacher," Chief Okibe said.

"Greetings to the father of the house. Greetings to the honourable Chief, the great benefactor of our people," Teacher said.

"Please sit down and feel at home. What would you like to drink?" the Chief asked.

"Anything you offer me, Chief," Teacher answered.

"Well, I can offer you beer, whisky, gin, brandy and something I bought when I was last in Portugal, called Porto. It is very sweet and needs to be taken very cold, if not slightly chilled. It is now my favourite appetiser," the chief added.

"OK Chief, I'll go along with the Porto. So how are all the members of your family?" Teacher asked.

"Well, most of them are at the moment abroad. All my children are either studying or working abroad, two in the UK and three in the USA. My wife is currently in our house in London. I have asked my Ibibio houseboy to make some pounded yam with egusi and bitter leaf soup for us," the Chief announced. He then called the houseboy and asked him to bring the bottle of Porto from the refrigerator with two wine glasses.

"So, I hear you would like to continue the good works of the late Chief Ogori. It is good that very able and experienced sons of the soil are prepared to sacrifice themselves for the good of the community," the Chief declared.

"It is not a sacrifice to wish to lead," Teacher responded.

"Yes, that is true. But you won't be an ordinary type of

leader. The moment you ascend to the throne, you don't belong to yourself anymore. You don't belong to your family anymore. Your physical body will be replaced by a sacred one, because you will be considered as part of the world of the dead and departed. Only a small number of authorised people can approach you, sit next to you, speak with you. There are things you will no longer be allowed to do in public. Should a member of your family die, you won't be allowed to go and see his or her dead body and take part in his or her burial, because you are part of the dead, and the dead do not meet in this world of ours. When there is a public gathering, such as the new yams festival, you will be required not to show the sentiments you may have as a man, such as laughing when you watch something funny, frowning when you see something that is but shouldn't, and of course crying when you watch something sad and moving. You and your body will belong to the village. If you are chosen, you will spend ten days in isolation in a hut within the village shrine. You will face lots of trials during this period. Only the Otse Arekwu and the Ada Agila can come and talk to you, from outside the hut. It is them who will bring in the meals your wives would have prepared for you. Nobody is to see your face during this period, not even the Otse Arekwu and the Ada Agila. Your physical body will die during this period and when you successfully emerge from your isolation, you will be emerging from the land of the dead, the land of the departed. Your head should never be uncovered, even when you are at home. You should always wear the special red and yellow cap that will be made for you. When you address people, you should not speak too loudly. People should be very quiet when you speak. This means that you should not repeat a question that you ask someone who comes to you for advice and guidance. And of course, manifestations of anger are totally out of the question. Anger is reserved for humans, not for those who live in the world of the departed. So, that's about the fundamentals. Do you still wish to go ahead?" the Chief asked.

"Yes, more than ever," Teacher replied. "It would be an honour to serve our people. It is crucial to get the local, state and federal governments better aware of the needs of our people and to put pressure on them to bring electricity and potable water to the village," he added.

"It is important to be ambitious. What you will need to do first and foremost is to bring peace to the village, to maintain unity in our community and to iron out border difficulties with the Ezas. You will have your hands full," the Chief contended.

"Our history with the Ezas is full of ups and downs. I will do all that I can to make sure there are more ups than downs in the future," Teacher replied.

"That is a good start. I will inform the Ada Agila that the council should start making the necessary arrangements for your traditional ascension. Let us now go to eat, Ogaba Idu. One last thing. I'm told one of your sons is in prison in Otukpo. I will make the necessary arrangements for him to be released this week. That way, your ascension will not be polluted," the Chief went on to say.

"Thank you, Chief," Teacher answered.

Teacher was in the house built by his brother in the village when all the members of the Council of Chiefs came to visit him. This house would become the chief's palace. But before then, what had to be done had to be done. Teacher was going to be escorted when it was dark, and when everyone else was sleeping, to the village shrine. The shrine was close to the patch of forest from where all the masquerades emerged. There were three round huts in the shrine, arranged one after the other in a straight line each separated by a batch of tall palm trees. The first hut was where the masquerades that entertained the village during happy festivals, such as the new yams festival, usually emerged from. The second hut was where those masquerades that only appeared when titled elders and members of the Council of Chiefs passed away emerged from. The third hut was a no-go area. This was where men who were chosen to lead the village and head the Council of Chiefs had to stay for ten days and converse with the departed. This hut was constructed on the site where the first king of Agila had been buried. All three huts were surrounded by a fence made up of dry palm tree leaves. A small narrow path led to the fence. On each side of the path were huge trees with very large branches, some of which acted as roadblocks. Those going into and out of the shrine had to bend down in order to go under the branches and continue their visit into or out of the shrine.

Three members of the Council of Chiefs were absent when this body escorted Teacher at midnight to the shrine. The Otse Arekwu, the religious guide, led the way with a bush lamp, and he was followed by Teacher, with the Ada Agila or Prime Minister following closely behind. The religious guide was singing in a low guttural voice. He was imploring the ancestors to be prepared to receive a new member and to offer him all the intelligence they had acquired about worldly and non-worldly matters to make him a great leader of the community. The procession went past the first hut and then past the second hut, where the religious guide stopped. He told Teacher that he would have to go to the third hut all alone.

Teacher would have to find his way into the hut in total darkness since the religious guide was not going to give him the bush lamp. He wished Teacher long life and quickly left the shrine with the other members of the council.

Teacher was stuck for a few minutes. He waited a few other minutes to get his eyes used to the dark and get a bearing on where he was exactly. There were questions he would have liked to ask the religious guide which he had not had the time to. Would the door to the royal hut be open or closed? Was there a bed? Was the pit latrine far from it? He took a tentative step forward and then a second and then a third. He stretched his arm in from of him to touch the trunks of the tall palm trees that stood on either side of the path. Then he remained still. He thought he had heard some feet shuffling in front of him. He listened attentively but heard nothing. Then he took another step forward and stopped suddenly. Something was sliding on his feet, passing from one side of the path to the other. It was heavy and long and had a cold contact with his skin. He allowed it to finish crossing the path before he continued. Suddenly, the shrine was full of nightly activity, with dozens and dozens of bats shrieking noisily and excitedly, flying in different groups from one palm tree to the other. Teacher's outstretched hands touched the thatched roof of the royal hut. He found the door, opened it and fell directly on a bed made of dry clay. His hands went round the bed to determine its size. The bed was in the form of a coffin. As he was about to get up, he suddenly heard a child wailing. The voice sounded very familiar. The wailing was deep and unending, and Teacher was unable to sleep. Each time he was about to doze off on the clay bed, the wailing would become more strident and Teacher would open his eyes with difficulty.

He spent his first night awake, listening to the voice of a child wailing sadly. The second night was also one Teacher spent awake. This time around, it was the sound of someone dragging his feet around his hut which kept him awake. The person seemed to have several heavy metallic chains and some bells tied to his feet. His walk was thus accompanied by a loud noise of bells and the clanging of chains. The third night was more challenging. Teacher could not sleep because a very pungent smell filled the hut. It was the smell of rotten flesh, the smell of death. The fourth night was the most challenging for Teacher because a swarm of mosquitoes preyed on him. There was nothing he could do but allow them feast on his body. He thus stopped struggling and trying to kill them with his hands. Then he finally fell into a very deep sleep. He found himself in a dark narrow tunnel with light at the other end. The closer he got to the light, the farther it went. Groups of mosquitoes were chasing him, so he walked faster in order to outrun them. He did not run. Then he reached the other end of the tunnel and saw a big wide river with brown water flowing slowly.

On the other bank of the river, he saw someone who looked like his father inviting him to swim across the river and join him. He knew he could not swim but the opportunity to talk again to his father made him jump into the river, which suddenly started to flow more rapidly. He felt his strength waning, felt himself sinking slowly into the rushing water, tried to hold his breath for a moment, before finally losing control. He did not know how long he had been under the water but when he woke up, he was in a very wide white room. There were many people in the room, all dressed in white agbadas. Many of them looked familiar. There was one that resembled his father. He tried to make eye contact with him, but this was not possible because the man had no eyes. What he had were two gaping holes where the eyes should have been. Then he noticed that only men were in the room. Where were the women? All the men were moving slowly, shuffling their feet silently. Then they all stopped. Teacher understood why because at that moment appeared a tall thin white bearded man with extremely white teeth, dressed equally in immaculate white agbada.

All the pairs of eyes that were not eyes turned towards Teacher, staring at him. The bearded man walked towards Teacher, took him by the hands and led him to another room. He asked Teacher why his body was hot, and Teacher said he did not know why. He touched Teacher's face and wiped the sweat on it. He showed the wet piece of cotton fabric he had used to Teacher, who was alarmed to see that it was wet with blood. He then dipped his hands into a basket and brought out a peacock. He placed his right hand on the peacock's breast and plucked out the peacock's heart, which was still beating slowly. He gave the raw heart to Teacher and ordered him to swallow it, blood drenched. Teacher swallowed it with difficulty.

Suddenly a flash of pain struck his chest. He bent over, holding his stomach. The bearded man put him in a foetal position and started rubbing some oil on his body. Some oil droplets fell on the floor and Teacher was alarmed once again when he saw that the oil was in fact a very dark reddish blood. Then he covered Teacher from the shoulder down his thighs with a piece of red and yellow wrapper made of cotton. Teacher began to shiver uncontrollably. He felt himself dozing off slowly. He tried to remain awake, but the call of sleep was stronger. So, he let go, and found himself floating over the village. He knew it was the village but was unable to say exactly which sector of the village or whose compounds he was watching from above. Then he heard a faint sound, coming from afar. The sound came nearer, and he was able to make out the beat and rhythm of a drum beating. Then he heard the sound of a second drum, which was very low-pitched. The low-pitched percussive sound continued as he thought he heard a voice from far away asking Ogaba Idu to come back from the land of the departed ancestors and join the living. It was the voice of the religious guide. He opened his eyes and saw that he was still lying on the clay bed in the hut which was pitch dark. This was the tenth and final night he had spent in the royal hut. He was ready to lead his village.

Teacher's coronation celebration lasted an entire week. Cows were slaughtered and goats slain for the village to eat as much as they could. Various types of drinks were served to people who flocked to Teacher's residence. People ate and drank. Teacher was happy. He loved it when visitors knelt down in front of him, singing songs of praise and wishing him eternal life. He enjoyed the deference his mere presence now generated. He liked to see the many women that came to greet him, going flat on their bellies, pouring eulogies on him and wishing him a very long and satisfactory reign. He observed the constitution of a group of court jesters and hangers-on, who spent the whole day sitting around him, greedily eating and drinking what was offered to them. He saw the numerous vehicles that transported the sons and daughters of the village who lived not only in the cities of Otukpo and Makurdi but as far away as Abuja that thronged the front yard of his residence. These worthwhile sons and daughters of the village had come to pay him homage. Some came with goats. Others came with hens, cocks, ducks and peacocks. Two came with cows. Many others brought cartons of beer, crates of soft drink, bottles of wine, whisky and gin. Some others came with wads of banknotes, which they humbly gave to Teacher, wishing Ogaba Idu long life, and great wisdom so that he could lead the village peacefully. It was Chief Okibe from Abuja who really showed his strength to the village: he brought three cows, ten goats, several cartons of beer and a very fat wad of banknotes.

Teacher loved it when he saw the air of great reverence that all who came to pay him homage had as each stood with their hands behind their backs when they spoke to him. He saw the excitement that was on the faces of everyone knowing that the village would now be led once again, after more than six months of power vacancy. What Teacher did not see was the work done by the womenfolk. Enotse had been able to mobilise more than a dozen other women to prepare the meals that were served all day long. They worked relentlessly to ensure that there was always something to be served to visitors. They sweated near the fire, were quick to fan the fire with a fan made from the leaves of palm tree and did not complain of the blue smoke that sometimes blinded their sight momentarily. Teacher was happy that the flow of food and drinks was uninterrupted. He would have been happier and extremely contented if his second wife had been around in the village to witness this great week.

Orinya had decided that she was not going to spend an entire week in the village breaking her backbone and allowing smoke to enter her eyes just because her husband had become the Village and District Head. She had been told her husband had disappeared into thin air, was in isolation with the ancestors and that he would reappear ten days later. It would be normal for his wives to be with him when he emerged from his spiritual journey. She had countered that her presence in the village would add or subtract nothing from what had been ordained. What would her spending ten days idle waiting for her husband to emerge add to the success of his coronation, she wondered. Was the waiting not the privilege of the first wife, she questioned. Nothing anybody said had convinced her that her place was with her husband, Ogaba Idu, so she remained in Otukpo all the time her husband was being celebrated in the village. There was much talk around the village. Who else but a witch could decide not to partake of the joy that united the entire village community? Who else but a wicked witch would choose not to witness the re-birth of her husband from the land of the dead? Who else but an evil witch would prefer the easy life in the city, and abandon her duty to feed the village, in her capacity as a wife to Ogaba Idu, leader of the village, the light of the district, the bringer of prosperity to all and the protector of its inhabitants? Come to think of it, who else but a woman like that could mother a son who was a renowned criminal? By the way, why had the son been released from prison before the term of his sentence had expired? Maybe both she and her son were in the city planning evil together.

Teacher had his hands full. His residence was full of people who came to ask him for advice, for financial help, or for his assistance on different matters. Teacher was always surrounded by the other members of the Council of Chiefs. He soon noticed that three members of the council were always disagreeing with actions he chose to do or decisions he chose to make and apply. He learnt that all three had been against his candidacy for the stool and that each had received a Honda 175 motorcycle as present from the Ogori family. Teacher did not even try to speak to them individually so as to get to know them better and to try to allow them to get to know him better. Rather, each time they spoke during the meeting of the council, he would speak to them with a very condescending tone, telling them that they did not know what they were talking about or that their comments were irrelevant to the questions being addressed. The first challenge to his authority came when his father-in-law, Orinya's father, passed away. He informed the council of his intention to go to the father-in-law's compound in order to pay his last respects and condole the family.

"This is completely out of the question. It is unheard of and unthinkable," one of the three rebels said vehemently.

"You don't need to be vehement and full of ire when what I want to do is understandable to all who are capable of thinking," Teacher responded with undisguised disdain.

"Your predecessor, Ogaba-Idu Ogori, the gods bless his name and memory, would never have even thought of what you are planning to do, let alone announce it publicly. You should seek advice from seasoned people in the council before imagining such unroyal actions," the man continued.

"You don't know what you are talking about. What is unroyal in my wanting to say good-bye to the father of my wife?" Teacher asked, incredulously.

"The dead do not go to meet the dead. You are no longer your wife's husband but the husband of the entire village. You are no longer part of us, the living, but a spirit sent by our departed ancestors to lead us through the many difficulties that

197

face us. The dead do not meet the dead, the result will be catastrophic for the village. Locusts will come and destroy our farms. Our river will overflow and flood the village. The winds will blow very strongly and uproot all our palm trees. The gods will get very angry and we don't know what plight they will send to us as punishment. No, you cannot go to see who you call your father-in-law off, because both of you are already together. Is what I'm saying right or wrong, Otse Arekwu, our religious guide?"

The religious guide spoke in a whisper and confirmed what the councillor had just said. It was unthinkable for the Ogaba-Idu to go and see a dead body, even if it were the body of his child or any close member of his family.

Orinya said she would never forgive her husband for failing to attend the burial ceremony of her father. Teacher sent some emissaries to her to explain his quagmire, but she continued to bear him a grudge. How come he was always wanting people, and particularly his wives, to be at his service with unflinching loyalty, yet was incapable of understanding and accompanying their grief and sorrow? Did he feel completely on top of the world now that he was surrounded daily by people pouring him eulogies? Did he not understand basic human feelings of pain, sadness and grief?

Teacher's ambition was to climb from being the Village and District Head of Agila to being the head of the entire Idoma tribe, the Och'Idoma. He would then live in the vast government-built palace in Otukpo, capital city of the Idoma people. The Och'Idoma was a first-class chief, unlike the District Head who was only a third-class chief. Not only was the emolument paid by government higher, but the influence wielded by the Och'Idoma was much stronger at the state and federal levels. Teacher knew he had an advantage when compared to the other District Heads who would vie for the Och'Idoma stool once this became vacant. He was the only District Head that had a post-secondary university education. He thus arranged to be invited once in a while by a radio station based in Otukpo, where he responded to various questions on local, state and national affairs.

Enotse had never complained in her life. She had always stood by her husband and had willingly sacrificed her life to devote herself to him. She was now respected by the entire village as the Ogaba Anya, meaning the queen of women. People around her said admiringly that she was a strong woman. She was thought to be full of energy, never stumbling in her duty to maintain the royal household as it should be. Did anyone who went to visit the village head during lunch or supper time leave empty-stomached? Was her generosity not legendary? She never complained in her life except now.

She told her husband she was not feeling very well and that she needed to go to the general hospital in the city of Otukpo. She had telephoned their son in Funtua to tell him how she was feeling, and he had advised her to hurry urgently to the hospital in the city. When she informed Teacher, he said her going to the hospital could wait because a group of policemen were arriving from the city to visit him and help him solve the incessant crises the village had with the Ezas. It was unthinkable that they should visit him and not be fed as was befitting of his royal station. When she informed him that their son, who was a medical doctor, had sounded alarmed and almost ordered her to go the city hospital, he retorted that their son was being unnecessarily negative. He said he was nevertheless going to send for the nurse who worked in the village dispensary to come over and asked her to make sure his police guests were well catered for.

Enotse spent the whole day cooking. She was sweating very profusely, but she continued sitting near the fire, looking over the yam that was boiling and the egusi soup with goat meat she was preparing. It was after the policemen had been served and were discussing noisily that Enotse fell down and collapsed outside, near the fire. She was taken into her bedroom, placed on her bed with someone fanning her rapidly, while the village nurse was quickly sent for. When the nurse arrived, Enotse was in a coma. The nurse took her pulse and said she was going to remain with Enotse and look after her during the night. She needed to be transported to Otukpo the following morning, by which time she would hopefully have woken up. Enotse was at the hospital for a long period during which she underwent a whole battery of tests. She was advised not to engage in too much physical effort. She was told to take things easier. She was told to rest and replenish her energy. Why not go to live with one of her children working in the north? There, she would have nothing physically exhausting to do, no cooking to handle, no visitors to entertain, no more wahala in life, how did she feel? She said that was not the life meant for her. She was now Ogaba Anya, and her place was in the village with her husband.

During Enotse's absence, Orinya agreed to go to live in the village with her husband. The number of daily visitors to her husband's residence started to diminish dramatically. People did not want to eat meals prepared by someone many considered a witch. Orinya's bearing was not very warm and welcoming. People said she was arrogant, that she thought of herself as half Oyibo, given her light complexion and her permed hair. People complained she did not return their greetings. People regretted the absence of Ogaba Anya. Orinya was furious each time she heard a visitor ask her husband when Ogaba Anya was going to come back to the village. One day, her son, Sonny, came from Otukpo to visit her in the village. He showed reverence to his father but was quite rude to many of the visitors especially those who dared to ask him what he was now doing with his life. Teacher told him that such a behaviour was unbecoming of the son of a chief. Sonny said he would soon leave the village anyway and go back to the city, where more civilised people lived. Sonny left one day without saying goodbye to his father. Teacher was apprehensive because he suddenly had the feeling that something was amiss. He went into his bedroom, normally forbidden to all in the house, and discovered that the big wooden box in his bedroom where he kept all his money had been smashed open. He called his wife and accused her calmly of working closely with her son to bring shame to his name. Orinya replied that if he had been with her son when the latter was growing up, he would not be what he had turned out to be as an adult. She told him that rather than accuse others of their failings, one should be humble enough to accept and acknowledge one's own failings. The monkey who does not see his swollen anus laughs at the swollen anus of other monkeys around him. She told him that the word "humble" was certainly one he had never applied to himself. She reminded him that a leopard does not give birth to a goat and that the son of a vampire will always like the taste of blood, like his father.

A few days after Orinya left the village for the city, Teacher felt a slight pain in his chest. This was strange. It was the first time ever that he felt there was something heavy weighing down on his chest. Then he started getting tired very quickly. He now spoke more slowly, as the effort to speak seemed to use all the energy he had. He would stop speaking in the middle of a sentence, and pant for his breath slowly before resuming on the topic he was on. Enotse, his wife, was worried. What had he been given to eat during her absence, she would ask? Could he remember a day when what he had been given to eat tasted differently from its usual taste, she questioned. She called her son in Funtua, who advised her not to panic. It was normal, he said, for his father to have difficulty speaking loudly, quickly and continuously as he was wont to in preceding years, because he was now much older. He promised to contact the village nurse and give her instructions about how to visit his father regularly to check his blood pressure, his temperature and his general health.

The Council of Chiefs was now very deeply divided. Over half of its members were dissatisfied with how village problems were solved. Many were particularly unhappy with the image of weakness they felt the Ogaba Idu was giving to the belligerent Eza neighbours. The three pro-Ogori councillors believed that Teacher was getting a swollen head because of some of the achievements he had been able to make for the village. The village was now linked to the national power grid and there was thus electricity for four hours in the morning and four hours in the evening. Teacher had also been able to have the state government construct a borehole in the village. This provided potable water for all. The three councillors felt Teacher now took himself to be a first-class chief, rather than the third-class chief that he was. They were thus very willing to join other councillors to question how

Ogaba Idu thought of resolving the crises with the Ezas.

There was stalemate when three Agila hunters were killed during a hunting expedition in the bush a few kilometres away from the village. The bush was officially Agila land. Many in the village thought the hunters had to be avenged if Agila did not want to give the Ezas the impression that Agila land could be taken and seized at will by its neighbours. This was the stance that many members of the council wanted to take. Teacher told them that a punitive expedition to avenge the death of the three hunters would have dire and uncontrollable consequences. He informed the council that he had a few spies here and there in Eza land and that he had been informed that the Ezas possessed many sophisticated weapons. He said what was needed was restraint rather than violence. He was going to contact the state government in Makurdi to ask competent state authorities to intervene.

The three pro-Ogori councillors contested such a move, saying that more villagers would be killed before someone from the state accepted to come to serve as an intermediary between the village and its neighbouring Eza communities. Teacher was however able to convince most of the councillors that restraint rather than a call to arms was the better method of managing the inter-communal crises.

A few months later, three Eza men were caught red-handed uprooting yams in a farm that belonged to an Agila man. One of them tried to shoot those who captured them. They were brought to the residence of the village head for him to decide their fate. Teacher let them go, unharmed. Teacher learnt from his spies in Eza land that groups of young armed men were being organised here and there to come and harass people in Agila village. He decided to organise groups of young men who were armed and posted as sentries outside the village, in various locations. These were empowered to control those who entered the village. Unknown faces were questioned and some of them turned back when they failed to give adequate and convincing reasons for their visit to the village.

This system of sentries worked quite well, because no one was able to launch an attack on the village. There were skirmishes now and then. Gunshots were heard in the village. The village elders listened each time and declared that the loudest shots were those unleashed by the village sentries. Then one day, a group of sentries was attacked and their bodies beheaded. The three pro-Ogori councillors said the fault was Teacher's. They had watched his stamina gradually diminish and felt he was allowing his personal physical weakness and manifest failing health tell on his capacity to protect the village. Teacher had stopped going to the radio station in Otukpo to share his thoughts on state and national affairs. He now spoke very slowly, sometimes with difficulty. But he believed he had a duty to perform: guide his village in such a way as to avoid an open war with neighbouring Eza communities. The traumatic Biafran war was long forgotten and its wounds painstakingly healed. Engaging in a new war would open a Pandora's box with unimaginable negative consequences, lots of suffering and uncountable unnecessary deaths.

13

"I think I gave her too much freedom," Teacher whispered.

"Gave who?" Enotse asked.

"Mama Sonny. I wanted her to feel at ease in my home and she took that as meaning she could behave like a child and seek to be the man in my house," he replied after a minute of silence.

"Feeling at ease does not necessarily lead to the dereliction of one's duty as a wife and as a mother. Being married brings out the real character of someone. You know if the person thinks only of himself or herself. You know if the person is ready to forego his or her desires so that the wellbeing of those he or she lives with - husband, wife, children, stepchildren, in-laws and close relatives — can be guaranteed. Some are born to be married while many others are not, even though they do not know this," Enotse continued.

"I have always wanted to have a big family. I thought I had been able to have one. What went wrong?" he wondered in a low voice.

"It is not size that matters but the quality of relations you have with your family. There is a question I have been wanting to ask you for a long time. Have you ever thought of anyone else but yourself?" Enotse enquired.

"What kind of question is that," Teacher responded, frowning.

"I mean, do you really feel the pain and the suffering that

members of your family sometimes feel and have?" she continued.

"What kind of question is that?" he repeated, frowning all the more.

"Did you feel the pain I felt when we lost one of our twins a long time ago? You were busy trying to bring a girl young enough to be my daughter to my house to contest with me. Today, are you saying you did not know what you were doing? You say you gave her too much freedom. Is it today, now that you are lying on this bed, that you have suddenly seen the light? And why are you telling me this, anyway? What good will it do for you, for me and for our family?" she argued.

"Talking of the twin child, I think I heard him crying uncontrollably when I was at the royal hut," he announced.

"What did you do? Did you call his name?" she asked, looking at him intently.

Teacher avoided her gaze.

"No, I did not. He cried all night and I was unable to sleep," he responded.

"He cried all night because he was requesting for your attention and recognition. He wanted you to remember him, and he would have stopped crying the moment you called his name and told him not to cry anymore because his father was there to soothe him, understand him and take care of him," she informed him.

They sat in silence for some very long minutes.

"Talking about children, are you happy with how your children relate to one another?" Enotse asked.

"What do you mean?" Teacher responded, alarmed.

"As Ogaba-Idu who has tried everything to maintain the unity of the village and to avoid confrontations with our neighbours, are you contented to see and live with the enmity that has grown among your children, between my children and those of my housemate, to whom, as you have just said, you gave too much freedom?" she explained.

"The fact that they quarrel now and then is not abnormal you know. It is called filial jealousy. My own father had many children and we were all always fighting with one another. That did not prevent us from coming together when the need arose. That did not stop me from taking over the education of many of them," he responded.

"Filial jealousy should not lead to hatred," she affirmed.

"Are you trying to tell me I have failed in bringing up my children. This is quite funny because a white man I was discussing with when I was in Europe told me almost the same thing," Teacher continued.

"I am not saying you have failed in bringing up your children. I'm only saying you turned your eyes away when it was stark clear the filial bond that should unite your children was being openly smashed under your nose by the person you now say behaves like a child. You should have put things right when it was still possible," she maintained.

"You are certainly right. I have been thinking of late about what I have tried to achieve in my life and how I have tried to do this. I realise that I have always used my father as my guide, as my compass, as the model to follow in home-bringing. I have always held my father in awe. This was someone who each time he went to the bush always came back with some bush meat to feed his very large family. This was someone who was fearless, whom all other titled elders held in high esteem. This was someone who had the biggest farm of all. I have always wanted to live up to his expectations, and to be able to match his achievements. I never discussed or chatted with my father, neither did any of my other brothers and sisters, by the way. I just wanted him to be proud of me, to acknowledge my presence around him, to call me by my name, like I think all of his children craved for. I was elated when he chose that I be the first to go to school in order to learn the language of the white man, so as to better protect him. It appears that I have been struggling all my life for my father's approval, rather than take care of my children. I have, for example, pursued the objective of becoming the Village and District Head to be like my father and hold an even higher chieftaincy position than him. The result is the bad medicine my opponents have given me to eat and drink, which has led to this illness that I now have. So, you think that what has gone wrong is me, in me?" he wanted to know.

"Many things have gone right because you were there and wanted them to go right. Some things have gone wrong. It is difficult today to say if they went wrong because of you. What is clear is that you should have refused, as the father of the house, Mama Sonny's decision in Maiduguri that our children should no longer have their meals together. As a teacher, did you allow students to decide what to do in your classroom? I'm sure you did not. Now, we have a divided family. Why has none of my stepchildren come here to visit you? Because they don't want to set foot in Doctor's house, that's the only reason. Can you imagine that? They know their father is ill, many of them are in Abuja not far from here, and they refuse to come to their stepbrother's house to visit their father. What poison has their mother given them for them to behave in such a manner? They were not like that when they were very young," Enotse added.

"Mama Sonny used to complain that I was paying more attention to your children than hers. She said the result was that your children succeeded better at school than hers," Teacher added.

"Complain, did she? Have I ever complained? My children, our children, are not better gifted than my stepchildren. They have only worked harder. He who fishes with tact, precaution and perseverance does not leave the river empty-handed. Almost all my stepchildren are like their mother, who spent many years staying at home, doing nothing, and waiting for you and others to provide food and clothing for her and her children. The farmer who makes the effort to bend down and till the earth even when the weather is bad is sure to have a bountiful harvest," Enotse responded.

"I see what you are driving at, but I don't want to quarrel with you now. She said she did not feel appreciated in her worth, that visitors to the house held you in higher esteem than her," Teacher confided.

"This explains why she once told me she did not think our house was hers. What did she expect, that she would become the mistress of the house and me become the second wife?" Enotse asked.

"I have always told her to respect you as her elder. I have always told her to ask for your advice in doing things, in educating her children, in managing the house. But you know she is so strong-headed. This was not the image she gave when she was younger," Teacher said.

"I do not know what you told her. What I know is that her children stopped respecting me once they saw their mother's behaviour towards me, and once they saw that you, their father, appeared to condone their behaviour. I refused to want to be the man in your house and to tell you what you should have done to arrest the drift in the wrong direction," Enotse continued.

Teacher coughed for a long time. He began sweating. He stopped talking for some time in order to regain his strength and breath. He looked intently at his wife, with a very sad and far-away look. He cleared his throat twice.

"I have always wanted to have a big family," he said after a long moment of silence.

"I have always wanted to have a big family too. I am lucky, we are lucky to have been blessed with children, with lots of children. I have always thought that bringing them up to respect themselves and respect others was primordial. I assumed that you shared the same perspective," she mused.

"It is something I share, of course," he answered.

"Then why did you turn your face the other way when this principle was being openly questioned by your second wife?" she asked.

"Maybe I was blind. Maybe I thought the consequences would not be too serious or damaging. Maybe I was too busy thinking of other things," he replied.

"Thinking of other things? I know and respect your ambition, your desire to be a better teacher, your desire to serve, and other qualities. You have always been thinking of tomorrow rather than appreciate what you have now, what you have today. This means you are absent today because your focus is on what tomorrow holds for you. As a primary school teacher, you are already thinking of when you will leave the primary school for a teachers' training college. As a teachers' trainer in the college, you are already thinking of when you will leave this post for something higher. As the village and

District Head of Agila, you are already thinking of when you will become the powerful Och'Idoma. So, rather than appreciate what you have today, you are in dreamland, waiting for a tomorrow that may be far worse than today. You seem to be a traveller, always drifting from a real world to an imagined one. You therefore do not appreciate what you have. Here we are, in your son's clinic in Funtua. Here we are, with me at your bedside from very early in the morning to very late at night and what do you see? You don't see what is but what isn't. You don't see who is, but rather who should be, but in reality, isn't," Enotse complained.

Teacher was very quiet. He still had that sad far-away look. Gone was the quizzical alertness on his face.

"It is not that I do not see. It is rather that I am wondering what I have done wrong to warrant such an illness and such expression of ingratitude from all those I have helped to rise beyond their stations. I am also wondering what will happen when I go to join my father. This is why I am asking you to forgive her. Do not think I do not see. I see very well. In reality, Mama Sonny holds you in high esteem, even though she herself does not wish to openly show this. She knows that your being called the Ene Ole or Ogaba Anya corresponds to what you are in reality. She sees the respect people give to you spontaneously and I think she somehow wishes that such respect should also extend to her. What she has failed to admit is that if you put a pot full of holes in the river, it will not float but sink. She has tried to draw attention to herself by being your exact opposite. Childishness, nothing but childishness," Teacher digressed.

"What I'm afraid of is what will happen when you go to join your father, as you say, which I know will not be soon.

There will surely be a problem with ownership of the house in Otukpo," Enotse said.

"As a matter of fact, apart from the house, there are some plots of land I acquired in the Government Residential Area (GRA) in Otukpo. Then there is also the very large expanse of land which used to be my father's, whose ownership I have been able to officially transfer to my name. The problem is that the documents concerning the plots in Otukpo and in the village were part of what was stolen from my box by Sonny in the village. His mother tells me her son has nothing to do with the disappearance of the documents but I know he stole them, in addition to the huge sum of money that he took before running away from the village," Teacher answered.

"All my children are fortunately now working and have been able to build their own houses in the GRA. But I'm surprised to learn only today that you bought some plots of land in Otukpo. Was Mama Sonny aware of this? If she was, are you sure Sonny was not actually sent to the village to get the land certificates?" Enotse wondered.

"We will ask her when she comes. I know she will," Teacher responded.

"Do you expect her to tell you she has the documents her son stole from your room in the village? She is not child enough to openly admit being a thief in her husband's home. Anyway, you have not answered my question. Don't you think you should have informed me of your purchase?" she commented.

"Would you have agreed with me? You would have said I should rather build a house in the village next to my brother's, which as I said has become the family home," Teacher said.

"So, that means that Mama Sonny was aware of your

purchase. I now understand better why she sent her son to go to the village to obtain the documents. Are you sure the documents had your name on them? Do the land ownership certificates not bear her name, in reality?" Enotse wanted to know.

"I can't recollect. I am now not sure," Teacher responded in a low voice.

Enotse sat still for quite some time. The noise of the electric generator could be heard from afar and the ceiling fan was still squeaking now and then, as if it was crying in pain. The light in the room had been switched on. Then she saw her husband's body tremble slightly and realised he was sobbing quietly. She saw his saddened face, with drops of warm tears flowing slowly down his cheeks. Suddenly a very strong disagreeable pungent smell hit her nose. Her husband had been unable to control his bowels. Enotse soothed him, telling him in a soft gentle voice not to worry. Tomorrow would be a better day, she told him. She went to look for a bucket of water, a towel and some lavender perfumed soap. She delicately cleaned her husband's body, then used a cleansing lotion on it, something she had done a very long time ago, when her children were infant and unable to wash themselves, or take care of their personal hygiene.

GLOSSARY OF NIGERIAN 'LANGUAGE'

Abi?: A question tag. Isn't it? etc., depending on context. For example, **'Your name na Joe, abi?** = Your name is Joe, isn't it? '**You fit drive, abi?**=You can drive, can't you?

Aje butter: the socially well-off. The economically affluent.

Akamu: Pap (a traditional porridge or custard).

Anjenu: Ghost, Spirit.

Ashawo: Prostitute.

Bellyful: With your stomach full, no longer hungry, well-fed, satiated.

Bomboy: Baby boy.

Chei!: Unbelievable! Wonderful!

Egusi soup: Sauce made with ground melon and tomatoes.

Garri: Ground dry cassava. A staple Nigerian foodstuff.

Gra-gra: Trouble.

Gyara: Free offer of extra items.

Hear his grammar: Listen to his speech, Listen to what he is saying.

How you dey?: How are you?

I hear say: It is rumoured that, I have learnt from the grapevine that.

Iyanga: Pride, Arrogance.

Jalopy: Old and badly-maintained car.

Kai-kai: Strong local gin.

Kabiyesi: Your royal highness, His royal highness (among the Yoruba in Western Nigeria).

Koboko: Cane.

Mama Baby: The mother of a baby girl.

Mama Bomboy: The mother of a baby boy.

Moto: Motor car.

My old man: My father.

Na true you dey talk: What you are saying is right.

Na wa oh: This is surprising.

No be so?: A question tag. Isn't it? etc., depending on context. For example, '**Your name na Joe, no be so?** = Your name is Joe, isn't it? '**You fit drive, no be so?**=You can drive, can't you?

Oga: Sir, Master.

Ogaba Idu: Your royal highness.

O jarey: Please.

Original petrol; Unadulterated petrol or gasoline.

Oyiboman: White man, European.

Oyiboman no get legs: The white man doesn't have any leg.

Palava: Trouble, difficulty, Problems.

Particulars of vehicle: Vehicle papers (Insurance, Registration, Driving License).

Pickin: Child. **Small pickin**=Young child.

See am here: Here it is.

See as he get pointed nose: Can you see how pointed his nose is/looks?

Shakara: Arrogance.

Silencer: Exhaust pipe.

Show road pepper: Ply the road without breaking down.

To begin long grammar: To start a long speech.

To bleed well well: To bleed profusely.

To do iyanga: To show off with pride and arrogance.

To do iyanga like tolotolo: To be as proud as the peacock.

To do us gra-gra: To look for our trouble, to get on our nerves, to disturb us.

To eat something <u>fiam fiam</u>: To eat very rapidly, to gobble down quickly.

To give dash: To bribe or offer financial rewards.

To leave <u>now now</u>: To leave immediately.

To mess around: To be an unfaithful husband or wife.

To play shakara: To behave with arrogance.

To play sugar daddy: Old men who maintain young mistresses on whom they lavish gifts.

To quench: To die, to wither, to go off, to make disappear.

To speak in Naija: To clearly indicate to the person listening to you to give you a financial reward.

To talk jazz: To say stupid things. To exaggerate unnecessarily.

To yab: To say things. To speak. To talk. To engage in a conversation.

To vex: To become angry. To get annoyed.

Tolotolo: Peacock.

Wahala: Problems, Difficulties, Trouble.

Wetin: What.

Wetin you dey yab?: What are you saying? What are you speaking/talking about?

Why you dey yab like this?: Why are you causing such trouble/such anxiety?